Where the Water Is Cold

by James E. Ryhal

DORRANCE PUBLISHING CO., INC.
PITTSBURGH, PENNSYLVANIA 15222

ISBN 10: 0-8059-7281-1
ISBN 13: 978-0-8059-7281-8
Library of Congress Control Number: 2006924904

Printed in the United States of America

First Printing

For more information or to order additional books, please contact:
Dorrance Publishing Co., Inc.
701 Smithfield Street
Third Floor
Pittsburgh, Pennsylvania 15222
U.S.A.
1-800-788-7654
www.dorrancebookstore.com

To my father, James W. Ryhal,
who as a boy had an Airedale named Bum.

This is a true story. Some of the names have been changed.

Chapter 1

Iremember the first time I saw him. It was in the spring of the year, the last week of April, 1925. The colors of trees and bushes were everywhere. Apple blossom white, pink, and lavender swayed in the wind. Tulips and daffodils were in our yard. But the main attraction was the huge magnolia tree in front of our house. Many years an early frost had destroyed the blossoms, but not this year.

He stood under the huge magnolia, smelling the pink petals that covered the ground almost like snow. With his canine nose, the odor must've been wonderful. He was a young Airedale, perhaps nine or ten months old, certainly less than a year. He was a little thin and a little scraggly, with a year's growth of hair. He was black and tan, almost red, with a small patch of white hair on his upper chest almost to his neck. I guessed his weight to be between forty and fifty pounds.

There was a definite aloofness about him as he examined the petals from the tree and slowly surveyed our yard. He turned his head very slowly from our house to the Franklin's place next door. He glanced at everything around him in a very serious mood.

At last he saw me. He now stood motionless and nothing took his gaze away from me. A very serious look was on his face and I guess he wondered how long I had noticed him before he had noticed me.

I did not approach him, for his serious composure convinced me not to take liberties with him. For a short while we both stood motionless, looking at each other.

His independence became magnetic to me. I wanted to cross the yard to him, but I was definitely afraid. During all this time he never moved and I never even noticed his eyes blinking. I'm sure he knew I had fear of him. Dogs always seem to know this and he seemed very wise for his young age. He knew me better than I knew him.

After a short time I closed the distance between us. Regardless of what he would do, I started across the yard. Since I was in my own front yard, I

1

gained a little confidence. I walked slowly, but inside I was racing a hundred miles an hour. Halfway across the yard I was still frightened, but less frightened than when I started. Without any doubt, I knew he could see right through me.

At last, after what seemed like an eternity, I reached him. All this time he never moved. No moving of his head, no wagging his tail—nothing.

My left hand reached out to him and I placed it directly in front of his large black nose. He smelled it casually. I couldn't imagine what it smelled like, but he kept his nose on it a long time. His tail began to wag, slowly, very slowly, but it was moving. What seemed like the longest few moments of my young life passed, and I petted him, first with my left hand, then with both hands.

"Good boy. You are a good boy."

His tail moved a little faster and he knew I liked him. Now we knew we were no threat to each other. He continued to look around our yard as I continued to pet him. He never moved, but kept surveying everything to make certain that no one else quietly came up on him as I had.

After a short time I started around the side of the house to the back yard. He followed me. Expecting him to move on in his journey to somewhere else, I was surprised.

I wondered from where he had come. He had no collar and no dog license. Where was he from? Who had owned him? How far had he traveled? These things I would never know. He didn't seem concerned about the past either. If he had an owner, he certainly didn't indicate any loyalty to him now.

I stopped near the henhouse and he stopped with me. He looked at me, and staying near to me, seemed to show he wanted to stay.

I could not help wondering who this dog belonged to. Surely someone would come by and claim him. I'd never seen him anywhere before. Of course, I could never keep him. Dad might permit it but I would never get Mother's approval.

Mothers usually saw dogs as mud-covered wolves, created to soil carpets and chew up pillows. No, there was no way I could get her approval.

"Forget keeping him," I told myself. Even if by some miracle it could work out, someone would probably be along in a few days and claim him. "Forget it!" That's what I had to keep telling myself.

I started across the yard to Will Franklin's house. Will and I both lived on Moore Avenue, three blocks outside of New Castle, just outside city law. Will would probably be home and I hadn't seen him today. The dog followed me. Even though I showed no attention to him, he kept up with me.

Will slammed the back screen door.

"Got yourself an Airedale, eh?"

"No, Will. He's not mine."

"He's hanging around you like he's yours. He looks like he's thinkin' about stayin'."

"No, Will. He just came by. He's just a stray from somewhere."

"I kinda like 'im," said Will. "You could do a lot worse. He's a handsome guy."

This greatly interested me. Will Franklin knew a lot about dogs. He knew a lot about the outdoors, about wild critters, about fishing and tracking in the woods. Will knew about guns and shooting and all the things I was interested in. I always felt he knew about the things that really were important. Huckleberry Finn had surely been like Will Franklin.

"I gotta get to work, Jim," said Will. "I gotta cut our lawn or I'm gonna be in some trouble with my dad. I'll see you and your dog later."

For nearly two hours I waited in my own yard for my father to arrive home. My new friend lay in the grass beside me. Will Franklin was right. There was a handsomeness about him. With a comb, scissors, and some grooming, he could be very handsome.

It raced through my mind that he might even have a registered pedigree. I'd never know, but the possibility of it made it even more interesting that no one was looking for him.

· · ·

Our family car made its familiar sound as Dad drove over the gravel driveway into our garage. I hurried to see him and my new friend followed me.

"Dad, I want to talk to you," I said boldly, feeling very confident in my cause.

He looked at my new friend.

"Jim, I have a good idea what you wanna talk about."

"Dad, this is really important. It really is."

"Jim, I'm sure it is."

"Will Franklin said that this was really a fine dog. You know Will knows just about everything about dogs."

"Good, I'm glad Will likes this dog. I have no problem with Will keeping this dog. He already has two Blue Tick hounds."

"No, Dad, I don't mean that. I mean me. Every one of my friends has a dog but me."

"Jim, you'll never get this animal past your mother. I'll try to help, but I know you'll never get her to agree about this."

The back porch door slammed and my mother came from the house.

"I heard it all from the kitchen window and your dad is right. You will have no dog."

"But Mom, almost every friend I have has a dog. Most of the kids I know have a dog—some have two of them."

3

"The carpet will be ruined and he'll chew up all our pillows. He'll be a huge nuisance."

Now came all the familiar reasons and I'd heard them all a thousand times. I'm certain I could quote them faster and even better than she could.

"And what about the yard? He'll dig holes. He'll kill all the tulips and every flower we have. He'll lift his leg on every bush and tree. My little vegetable garden will be gone, too."

"Now, Mother," said Dad.

"Don't 'Now, Mother' me! We worked so hard on this grass. The grass looks so good. Our lawn is very green already for this time of year. It'll probably be our very best year with this new grass seed. He'll absolutely ruin all our work on this grass."

"Now, Dorothea," said Dad. "We're not raising grass. We're raising a son and we want to do it right."

My mother was stunned. There was total silence. She simply had no idea what to say. Dad had struck something. He had said exactly the right thing at the right time.

"All right," she said. "But he's not to be in this house. He's never to be in the house. Only in the coldest winter, and only in the cellar, will he be permitted inside. Get him a dog house or a chain or something outside."

I was overjoyed, but tried to hide it. If I got too excited she might change her mind. My dad had done it.

"And what if he belongs to someone? What if someone comes for him? What'll you do then?" she asked.

"He doesn't belong to anyone. If he does belong to someone, I'll just have to give him up."

"Why you would want an old scraggly hobo dog like that, I'm sure I don't know!" She started back into the house, then stopped and made a final comment. "You're responsible for him. Don't expect me to clean up after him. Don't forget! You're always responsible for him—always!"

She slammed the kitchen door behind her and my struggle was over.

Dad looked at me and smiled. He never said a word, just smiled and followed her into the house.

"Thanks, Dad," I said softly.

I should've thanked Mom too. She had changed her mind; well sort-of anyway, and let me have him. I would thank her later. I should've thanked her also for helping me think of a good name for him.

He was a scraggly hobo dog. And that gave me the idea for his name. I would call him "Bum." It was a good name and it fit him well. I would surely remember to thank Mom later.

Chapter II

The Neshannock Creek came down through New Castle from the northeast. I never knew exactly where its source was, but it was somewhere around New Wilmington, Pennsylvania. In that area the creek was called the Little Neshannock.

Some parts of the creek were so narrow you could almost jump across, while other parts were very wide. The current was usually fast, a little slower where it was wide. Except for six or seven deep holes, the creek was shallow, oftentimes only knee-deep.

In the deep holes were some large trout. We usually swam in those deep holes and sometimes fished them. The creek was always cold. July and August were usually the only months we swam—occasionally late June. It was not that the water was any warmer at those times, but the air was warmer. You didn't feel the cold so much when you came out of the cold water in late summer. We fished in April, but never swam in the Neshannock at this time of year. Some of the best trout fishing was in April and May.

The creek had a great deal of life in it. There were big chubs in the Neshannock. These fish were a little boney, but pretty good eating. Many rock bass were there also. You could always tell when you had a smallmouth on your line in the creek. They broke water often and put on a great show. People didn't call them "old scrap iron" for nothing. Most sportsmen felt a nice smallmouth and a good rainbow were, pound for pound, the best fighting freshwater fish alive. Of course, it was the trout that brought us back again and again to the Neshannock. The creek had brooks, rainbows and a few browns. We were not particular—we liked them all.

About half our catch we returned to the creek. The other half we ate— usually pan-fried. At our age, we definitely were not gentlemen catch-and-release fishermen. We fished with rods—not poles. Poles were something that were pounded into the ground. Yet, despite our age, we knew how to use the fly rod.

After passing through town, the Neshannock met the Shenango River south of New Castle. Where the two streams met they became the Beaver River. Below Rochester and Beaver, Pennsylvania, the Beaver flowed into the Ohio that had come north about twenty-five miles from Pittsburgh.

Neshannock and Shenango were Indian names, but I could never find anyone who could tell me exactly what they meant. Johnny McCann's father told me they were Seneca words. He said his grandfather had told him that, but he wasn't absolutely positive about it, either. The source of both streams always seemed to remain a mystery.

The Shenango was a completely different animal than the creek. It was a full-fledged river that at one time had boat traffic on it. It was wide, deep, dark, and even a little mysterious. It flowed to New Castle from the northwest, north of Sharon in Mercer County.

Occasionally we would see mallards or wood ducks on the Neshannock, but the Shenango was different. Entire flocks of ducks and geese would come and go on the Shenango.

In the fall of the year, teal, pintails, mallards, wood ducks, and Canadian geese would migrate south. In the spring months they would return to local lakes and ponds. Many water fowl continued up to Lake Erie and beyond to the far North. It was a great show the birds put on, particularly in the fall.

The fish were much bigger in the Shenango River also. The largemouth bass were abundant. Rock bass, bluegills, carp, huge catfish, and muskies were caught. With its greater width there were more deer, raccoon, muskrat, and even beaver on the river.

But there were no trout in the Shenango. Therefore, our gang had no trouble choosing the Neshannock first. We fished the Shenango, but not more than once or twice a year. Unlike the creek, the river was warm. We liked it where the water was cold.

•   •   •

It was a good day—nice and warm, but not hot. The trail went down the side of the hill, through the pines, directly to the Neshannock. This patch of woods had absolutely no other type of trees in it. The patch of woods was not very big, and no one ever referred to it as anything else but Pine Woods.

The temperature was actually cooler in the pines. No one ever gave me a scientific reason for it, but we were positive the temperature was lower in these pines.

There were five of us in the gang and today we were all together. Each of us had our own rod—Johnny, Will, Charlie, Rome, and me. We made our way down the hill toward the Creek.

Johnny was talking as we walked slowly down the rain-slicked hill. It was common for Johnny McCann to be talking. He was usually giving us an unsolicited story of something he had read somewhere. Johnny was a smart guy, but today we wanted to fish, not listen to him. This, however, did not stop him and he just kept talking.

"Jim, you get *Boys' Life* magazine, don't you?" asked John.

"Yes."

"Did you read this month's edition? There's some great stories in it."

"No—I didn't read it."

"Oh man, you really missed it! There's a great article in this month's magazine on rattlesnakes—timber rattlers."

"On what?" asked Will.

"On rattlers—rattlesnakes."

"Oh, Will, don't ask him," Charlie muttered.

"Don't matter, he'll tell us anyway, if he wants to," said Will.

"Listen, you guys, this was a great article. I'm not kidding. This was really good."

"Okay," I said. "Tell us."

"You guys know that snakes sun themselves on warm days. They're cold blooded and really need the heat from the sun."

"Everybody knows that," snapped Will.

"But I'll bet ya you didn't know about the male rattler."

"Okay, I give up! What about the male rattler sunning himself?"

"Well, when the female suns herself, the male lays off about ten or twelve feet from her. Sometimes he even lays in the shade, hiding and protecting her."

"And that's your great story," Rome scoffed. "I gotta give you credit, John. You sure can dream 'em up."

"No, it's the truth—really it is!"

"I think he's right, Rome," said Will. "I read somethin' about that somewhere. The more I think about it, the more I'm certain he's right. The male does protect her."

"Well, maybe he is," said Rome, rather philosophically. "I don't care now, because there's the creek. I only know I care about finding some trout."

Fifty feet in front of us we could see and hear the Neshannock. We could also smell it. I never knew exactly why you could smell water like that, but I was positive that you could.

The bushes parted as the path went straight to the water. The stones on the path were from the creek that flooded each spring.

Bum reached the water first. He waded into it, took a drink from it, and continued to survey it as we got out our rods and our gear. After a short while, Bum found a little inlet and lay down in the water. The water was about two inches deep—just enough to keep him cool on his stomach and chest. Several minutes later he went to sleep with his head resting on his front paws.

Mostly we used wet flies, but also salmon eggs or a piece of night-crawler. Whatever worked we used. Some fly fishermen would never use anything but a fly, but not us. We liked dry flies and, at certain times of the year, wet flies. Most of all, we liked the bait that caught the most trout.

I worked my fly rod watching the floating line drift from left to right in the current. Far to my left upstream, Johnnie, Charlie, Rome, and Will were each catching little brook trout.

"Hey, young fella, come 'ere."

I heard someone calling, perhaps to me, but I couldn't see anything or anyone so I kept fishing.

"Hey, young fella, come 'ere."

Behind me, Bum moved in the shallow water. His head was up. He had heard the voice also. He looked to our right—downstream. I looked down the creek where Bum stared and saw another fisherman. The stranger stood in the shallow water near the bank, dressed in rubber hip boots. He was a lean, gray-haired man and he motioned to me with his hand to come to him.

My line came in slowly. I was going to go downstream to see him, but I was not going to grab a snag by hurrying. When my line was retrieved I started down the Creek toward the old fellow. Bum came with me.

"Look at this, young fella," he said.

He carefully held up a tiny rainbow for Bum and me to see.

"Look at him!" he said.

A tiny hook with a red leader was hanging from the fish's mouth. Next to it was another tiny hook with a broken red leader.

"What is it?" I asked.

"Ten minutes ago I lost this little fish when my leader broke. This has got to be the same fish."

"How do you know that?"

"Well, just look at the hook's little red leader. The one in his mouth is exactly like the one that's broken. It's exactly like the ones I'm using. This fish broke my leader and ten minutes later hit my line again. These leaders are exactly the same. He sure must've been hungry."

"Wow," I said. "I've never seen anything like that before."

"I never did, either. I've fished the Neshannock for fifty years and never saw it or heard of it happening to anyone else."

When Bum and I got back to our spot on the beach, our friends were packing up their rods and gear.

"Did you guys catch any?"

"We caught four," said Johnny.

"I got one," said Rome. "They were all pretty small and we released 'em. Where'd you go anyway!"

I told them the story of how Bum and I had traveled downstream to see the old gentleman. From the details of the little red leaders on the hooks, they knew I was telling the truth. They were as amazed as I was. None of us had heard or seen anything like it. The same trout caught by the same fisherman in less than ten minutes.

When we had walked only about twenty feet up the stony path, Will threw both his arms straight out.

"Stop!" he screamed. "Don't anybody move! Don't move—don't take a single step."

"What is it?" I asked softly.

"Look!"

In the middle of the path on the warm stones, not more than ten feet ahead, was a coiled snake. Very slowly it moved its head, sunning itself. It had not heard us and was not alarmed.

"Follow me," said Will. "We'll circle around through these small bushes. We don't want to tangle with that thing!"

Slowly we parted the bushes before us. Turning to our left, we cautiously circled the snake on the path.

Then we heard it! It was the unmistakable sound of another rattler. We froze!

"Where is he, Will?" whispered Charlie.

"He's only about four feet in front of me."

"Will, what do we do?" I asked.

"Damn! He's gonna strike me. We gotta run like hell and right now!"

The rattler struck at Will and only missed him by inches. The five of us crashed through the bushes. The first row of growth was small and we pushed it aside easily.

But steadily the bushes increased in size. They were now over our heads and lashing at our faces. They cut and stung us, but we did not stop. After nearly a hundred feet we slowed our pace.

"Don't stop!" yelled Will. "You don't know where we are. Keep goin'! Keep goin'!"

We were very tired now and sweat rolled from us. We breathed heavily and all of us seemed to stop together. None of us spoke, but we all kept panting. After several minutes we were all right again.

"Where's Bum?" I asked.

"I don't know," said Johnny. "I thought he was with you."

"Did you see 'im, Will?"

"Nope. I thought he was with you, too. After we started runnin', I never saw 'im."

"You don't think that snake got him, do you, Will?" I asked, my voice showing my worry.

"I doubt it," said Will, still panting. "That rattler went for me, and when he missed me Bum probably took off runnin'."

"But did you see him?" I shouted.

"No. I didn't see him."

"I never saw him either," said Charlie.

We stood there wondering what had happened and hoping to hear Bum coming or just hear anything from the thickness.

Finally I yelled as loud as I could. "Bum! Come, boy, come. Bum, come! Bum, come here!"

Nothing. There was no sound. We continued to listen and I began to fear the worst.

"What do you think, John?" I asked slowly. "Did you see Bum anywhere?"

"I'm not sure. I think you ought to keep callin'. But I don't think we oughta go back, not through those bushes where we heard that rattler."

"I'm not goin', I'm not goin' back," said Rome.

"Bum, here boy! Bum, come here! Bum, come!" I called as loud as I could.

This time there was a sound. It wasn't much, but I thought I heard it. "I'm sure I heard something."

"You did hear something," said Will. "I heard it too. But be quiet. Keep listenin', keep listenin'!"

The little sound grew louder. We were completely silent and the sound came closer. We waited.

From between the bushes, Bum came. He was very dirty with mud in his beard and tiny sticks throughout his entire coat. Something hung from both sides of his mouth.

"Jim, what's that he's got in his mouth?" asked Charlie. "It looks like a piece of rope."

"It ain't no rope," said Will. "He's got that rattler! That's probably the snake that almost got me, and that snake sure is a dead one now."

Will reached toward Bum to get the snake, but Bum turned away. He would not stand still for Will. He would not give up his new trophy.

I called him, but he would not come to me. I called him again and he walked away. At last I screamed at him at the top of my voice for him to come. Finally he stopped walking away. He would not come to me, but at least he stopped walking so I could approach him.

Slowly I moved to him. I had never seen him act like this before. Very clearly, he wanted no one to have his snake.

I softly took hold of the snake with my right hand. It was clearly dead. Bum held it in his mouth. Softly with my left hand I patted his mouth.

"Release," I said to him. "Release, Bum, release." I kept hitting his mouth softly as I spoke.

At last he gave it up. He didn't want to, but he gave it up. Very reluctantly he let it go. As I held it away from him, he gave one last jump and snapped at it.

Every vertebrae in that snake's body was broken. The snake drooped from my hand like a piece of soft string.

"Will, how'd he do that? And how'd he keep from getting bit?" I asked.

"When that rattler missed me, he was straight out on the ground. That's when they're most vulnerable. That's sure enough when your dog grabbed him."

"But how'd he bust him up like this? That snake is a real mess!"

"He shook 'im. Once he got hold of 'im, he shook 'im and shook 'im. He shook that snake like a rag doll. Once he got hold of that snake, the ball-game was over. Bum never gave him a chance to do anything. Damn, I sure woulda liked to've seen it. That fight would've really been somethin' to see."

"I didn't wanna see it," said John. "I just wanted to get the hell out of there."

Will looked at the snake closely. "I think I can save this skin. Yes, I'm sure I can. I'll skin him out when we get back. Jim, do you wanna keep the skin?"

"No, you can have it."

The four of them, with Bum, walked about fifteen feet in front of me all the way home. Two of them talked constantly. Will talked about the snake-skin and Johnny talked about the female snake sunning herself. As the two spoke, Charlie and Rome just listened. Bum kept jumping the whole time, trying to get that snake from Will.

I was a lucky guy. I had four great friends and a great dog. Will was the greatest outdoorsman in the world. I never doubted for a moment that he could skin that snake. I was certain he was part Seneca. He had a nose like a Native American.

Johnny was the smartest guy in the world. Two hours earlier he had told us about the male rattler guarding the female as she sunned herself. Charlie, Rome, and I laughed at him, but no more. I would never doubt anything he told me again. Never.

Bum had gotten that rattler. Every so often, he would jump and try to grab that snake again from Will. The legend of Bum had begun.

Chapter III

I had known Rome Beltrone longer than anyone else in our gang. He lived just three blocks away and if I cut through the backyards and ran a good pace, I could be at his house in less than five minutes.

We had started kindergarten together. We were now in the seventh grade and we had been together in every class. We played basketball on the same team and swam together often. After Charlie Rudolph, Rome was the best tennis player in our group. Rome was also a sharp dresser. He wore nice clothing even to places he shouldn't have—like fishing.

His real name was Romeo, but no one in our group ever called him that. Only once had I ever heard him called Romeo and that was by his mother on the third call for him to come for something. You might think he would be teased for having Romeo for a first name, but he never was. Rome and I were also together in the same youth group at St. John's Lutheran Church.

We headed out one summer afternoon to our little hideout at the edge of the woods near the Henderson farm. The five of us were all together and, of course, Bum came along. The hideout wasn't much to look at. We had simply piled up some downed trees and old logs, making them into a triangle. There was no roof over it, but that made it much easier to look over the top for any stranger approaching. No one ever came to this place but us, but we were always diligent.

Rome watched over the top log and could see nearly a hundred yards in all directions. He told us we were alone and therefore we could relax.

From a small paper bag Rome took the little treasures he had brought. His father smoked these little Italian cigars and from time to time, Rome would simply help himself from the box. The cigars were nasty little devils. They were short and twisted like a corkscrew. They were dark, almost black. They reminded us of something that had been dipped in motor oil or road tar. They looked bad and tasted even worse. Why we smoked them was a mystery. We probably did because that was all Rome could get.

I had never smoked any tobacco before. Will and Rome had smoked nearly everything from cigarettes and cigars to corn silk. I didn't know about John and Charlie, but presumed they had smoked cigarettes at one time or another. I never mentioned my inexperience with tobacco; there was no reason to tell anyone, especially since I didn't want the reputation of being a complete novice.

For a long time no one spoke. We puffed on and on and after we finished the little cigars, we crushed them on the ground. We each lit a second one and smoked some more. The taste was wicked, but we were getting used to them; at least I thought we were.

I was feeling fine and then a strange thing began to happen. The trees in front of me actually started to move. They moved slowly at first and then a little more.

"Jim," said Will, "are you all right?"

"Of course I'm all right! What's the matter with you?" I did not mention my inexperience with tobacco.

The trees continued to move, only faster and faster. I knew something was wrong.

"Are you sure you're all right?" asked Johnny. "You don't look so good."

"You look bad, Jim," said Charlie.

"It's probably these cigars," said Rome. "They can be tough, especially if you're not used to 'em."

"There's nothing wrong with me, I tell ya. I can, I can . . . ."

Somehow I couldn't seem to speak anymore. The trees were moving in a circle – round and round. The whole world was spinning. I couldn't keep my eyes open. I was falling, falling! Crash – I bounced as I hit the ground. The weeds covering the ground were damp and felt good on my face. I could hear the others speaking, but I couldn't answer them or even open my eyes.

"I don't feel very good either," said Charlie. "My stomach is very bad. I'm gonna sit down with Jim."

Charlie tried to sit down, but he fell right next to me. We lay next to each other as if shot by the same gunman.

"I am really sick," said Will.

"Me too. I'm beginning to feel woozy," groaned Johnny.

"You guys smoked those cigars too fast," said Rome. "You smoked 'em way too fast—that's what's wrong."

"I am really sick," said Will.

Rome started to dig a hole. He began to bury all the evidence. Papers, cigar butts, matches, all were swept into the hole.

"Ooooh," moaned Will. "I am really sick, really sick."

"Oh, shut up, Will," barked Rome. "We've heard ya enough times–just shut the hell up."

Rome cleaned up our little hideout pretty well. There was no evidence remaining on the ground. I don't know what we smelled like, but I could guess.

Will kept moaning. We did our best to ignore him, but it wasn't easy. The four of us rolled around on the ground like four little piglets from a litter. Will kept moaning. It was awful.

• • •

An hour later we were all at Doc Snyder's office. The four of us lay on tables and Rome sat on a chair talking with the doctor.

"What did you boys have for lunch?"

"Hot dogs, doctor. Hot dogs. We all ate at the old diner," said Rome.

"And you're the only one that's not sick. That's a little unusual. Are you sure you feel all right?"

"I feel fine. I didn't eat any, no hot dogs for me. I just had a Coke, just a Coke."

Rome was lying his tail off, but so far it was working. We hoped he could just keep it up, and somehow the other four of us could get through this thing.

Will started his moaning again. Rome didn't say anything about it this time, but managed to give him an unfriendly look. Doc Snyder examined Will more closely than the rest of us. Each time he pushed on Will's stomach, he moaned louder.

"Miss Wilson, will you please come in here?" said the doctor.

I lay quietly on my table and kept my eyes closed. I presumed the others had their eyes closed also, but I never opened mine to find out. My mind raced for some way we could get out of this place. There had to be a way and somehow I had to think of it.

"Miss Wilson, call these boys' parents. Tell them they are here and I would like each of them to come to the office as quickly as possible."

This was the last thing any of us wanted to hear. Now we knew we must get out. We knew we must get out fast—before any of them even arrived.

"After you've called their parents, call the District Health Office in Pittsburgh. Tell them we might have some kind of food poisoning, or worse."

"Yes, Doctor."

Doc Snyder put a thermometer inside my mouth. He didn't say anything. He pushed on my stomach and I made a low moan. I wanted to look up and see what was happening, but I was afraid. I could hear his nurse had returned, but still kept my eyes closed.

"Doctor Snyder, I got in touch with the people at the District Health Office in Pittsburgh."

"What did they say?"

"They thought it was a good idea to call Harrisburg. They said I should call the State Health Department and get their opinion. It could be more serious than any of us think. Then they advised us to keep them under observation."

The whole show was flying out of control now. Maybe we could just get up and walk out. We could tell our parents we simply recovered. I worried if Will could even walk. He was so sick, if we left him he just might blab everything.

Again I heard the door open. This time I could no longer resist and opened my eyes to see. His nurse was back and had even more disturbing news.

"Doctor, several of the parents have arrived. They're in the waiting room now."

Oh no! That was the last thing we wanted to hear. Oh no! We'd have to go on with this now. Where it was leading us, I did not know.

"Did you call Harrisburg yet?"

"No, Doctor, but I will right now."

"Don't put it off! Call them right now!"

Will's mother and Charlie's parents came directly into our room. They went straight to Doc Snyder.

"I'm sorry, you can't stay here," said Doc Snyder. "You'll have to wait in the outer room. I'm sorry. Take them out, Miss Wilson."

"But Doctor, is this serious? What is it? Can't you tell us something?"

"I'm afraid we're not sure yet. We've got things under control and we'll know soon. Please, you'll have to go into the other room."

They left and Rome left with them. We had no worry about Rome. I knew he would tell them the right story. He had left his light jacket on the chair in our room, but no one seemed to notice but me.

Again the door opened and the nurse stood in the doorway. I wondered what the news would be this time. Was my mother or father there? It was becoming a nightmare in slow motion and we couldn't escape.

"I reached the Health Office at the capital in Harrisburg," she said. "They gave me a little information."

"Good. Did they give us any help, or should I call them?"

"You don't need to call, but they are concerned that it might be serious, since four of the five of them are sick. It is probably contagious. They advised me to keep the fifth youngster under observation, also. They think he'll probably show some symptoms soon. And they said they would call back later."

"Did they mention anything else?"

"Yes. They are also calling Pittsburgh and having them send up some of that new serum for us."

"Good. Miss Wilson, will you please get five syringes ready. We might as well be prepared."

Syringes? Contagious? Where is this going to end? What'll I do? How do we get out of here?

For a good period of time there was silence. I kept my eyes closed, and at the same time knew the others had heard it all as I did. Maybe one of them had some idea—I hoped so. It looked as though we could not keep this thing going much longer! Syringes—oh, no!

I was desperate now. I was fearful that I would simply break down in the face of that needle. I knew it must be a foot long! Would it be in my arm? No, never! It was simply too big! But my little rump couldn't take twelve inches of that thin steel. It had to be in the rump – I was too young to die, but I couldn't find any way out. I wouldn't even reach my fourteenth birthday. How many people would be at my funeral? Would Sally Burger miss me? Even the thought of no more homework did not give me any peace. This was my end.

"All right, boys, you can get up now," said the doctor with a rather firm voice.

Slowly we rose from our tables. The expression on his face was easy to read. We knew the game was over. Somehow he knew. He knew.

"Miss Wilson, will you come in here?"

"Yes I will," she said through the doorway.

"Call Pittsburgh and tell them we won't need any help. Tell them to keep that serum. Then ask them to call Harrisburg and tell them everything is fine."

"Are you certain, doctor?"

"I'm certain. You may go now."

He walked to the chair that held Rome's coat. He held it up for us to see.

"Whose coat is this?" he asked, looking directly at me.

"I—I—I don't know."

"You are sure you don't know?" he asked, all the time knowing I was lying.

"It belongs to Rome, sir. He's in the other room. He must've left it," I said.

He held up a single little Italian cigar. "And who does this belong to? It fell out of the pocket of that little jacket. I guess it doesn't really matter who owns it. We all know about the mysterious illness now."

Strangely I felt better now. It was all out. At least we wouldn't have to face those monster needles! We would all have problems when we got home, we all knew that, but they would not be quite as terrible as those needles.

"One more thing," said the doctor. "Who does the dog in the waiting room belong to?"

"He's mine, sir. I'm sorry–I'd completely forgotten about him. I'll be certain he leaves with me."

"Good. You can all go now."

I got Bum onto the leash and we all started for home. We breathed better, for it was over—well, almost over.

Chapter IV

A major agreement had been made when Bum came to live with us on Moore Avenue. My mother had designated only three places he could stay if he was to take up permanent residence. He would be tied up—more accurately chained up—to the front of the henhouse. He could sleep in the small room in the front of the henhouse, and in the winters he would stay in our basement at night.

Bum certainly didn't mind being chained up if the weather was moderate. He didn't object to the small room; it was warm and comfortable. Yet I'm certain he liked our basement the best.

Our cellar was large and well lit. With a couple of old rugs for Bum, the cellar was very comfortable. The first thing each morning, and the last thing at night before bedtime, I let Bum outside for between five and ten minutes.

I liked our cellar probably more than Bum did. Many school nights I'd read there and be with him. Sometimes he'd watch me read, but usually he'd simply sleep.

There was an old bookcase containing books about the Great War. I'd blow the dust off them and spend hours reading them and carefully examining the pictures. There were photographs of horses, biplanes, artillery pieces, battleships and strange-looking tanks. I particularly liked the generals in fancy uniforms and the Germans with their spiked helmets.

My Uncle Henry had been a doughboy in the Great War, but I never knew what a "doughboy" was. He came home to Cleveland in January of 1919. The following month he came to visit us.

For long periods of time, my father would talk with his younger brother. Henry was much younger than Dad and only twenty when he went to France in March of 1918.

On one of his visits, Uncle Henry left his rifle from the war with us. It was a model 19.03, Springfield Armory, U.S. Army. My uncle worried that he legally shouldn't have this rifle. Consequently he left it with Dad to avoid any possible trouble.

Dad quietly left the Springfield in the north corner of the cellar. The rifle was never fired after Uncle Henry returned from France. From the moisture in our cellar, rust slowly began to cover the piece. Small pits now slowly developed and the Springfield deteriorated. Even the rifle's leather sling began to rot.

Yet I really wasn't concerned about its condition. I just liked to hold it and look at it. It stood almost high as I did. It was heavy and I wouldn't have wanted to carry it all day as Uncle Henry had. It was a piece of history. I put it to my shoulder and pretended I was in the trenches. My imagination did the rest.

After working the bolt, I'd squeeze the trigger making a loud snap from the firing pin. With each snap, Bum's head would pop up to see what was happening. I dreamt of shooting deer and black bears. Usually after five or six clicks Bum lowered his head, realizing that nothing of importance was happening. I enjoyed the winter evenings in the basement with my books, the old rifle, and Bum.

I watched Bum as he stretched on the tiny rug on the cellar floor. He had changed greatly since that first day. He was confident and at ease. There was a laid-back side to his personality. He was not quarrelsome, yet when he was pushed he was formidable.

His appearance had also changed. He was very muscular, with a small waist and a huge chest. He was probably fifteen pounds heavier than he was that first day he came along. His head was long and handsome. He had become a very mature and powerful young male. I never knew who his parents were, but they were undoubtedly fine-looking animals.

Nearly every family in our neighborhood had their own henhouse. Everyone wanted eggs to sell and eat. Some families raised Rhode Island Reds or White Plymouth Rocks. Others raised New Hampshires or the quarrelsome little Bantams. We had White Rocks.

That night I put Bum in the little room in the front of the henhouse. The weather looked like rain and he would be better off there if the weather grew worse. Usually if the weather was pleasant, I'd simply chain him outside.

My room was near the henhouse at the back of the house. When Bum was chained, I could usually hear the rattle of the old rusty chain. Tonight I had heard nothing since he was in that small room.

I sat on the edge of my bed in my pajamas, looking at the stars from my lone bedroom window. How far they were from me! There were so many they were uncountable, beyond even my imagination.

The stars made me feel very small. My life on Moore Avenue was so tiny in this universe. The more I looked at the stars, the more insignificant I felt. It was frightening to me.

I no longer wanted to think about the stars. I would think only of my little world with parents, with friends, with Bum, and the creek. In this world, I knew who I was and I was glad.

I pulled the light blanket over me as I crawled into bed. I was tired, closed my eyes and would be asleep soon. Our gang was going to the creek tomorrow and I would dream about the creek and about catching giant rainbows. My eyes were heavy and morning would soon be here.

A sharp cracking noise outside my window startled me. I stayed motionless in my bed and kept my eyes closed, hoping I would drift back to sleep. Again I heard it, but did not move. It was nothing. If I stayed motionless, I would drift back to semi-consciousness.

But the third time I heard it, I knew it would not go away. I opened my eyes and stared into the darkness of my small room.

What could be that crazy noise? It sounded like Bum was chasing something in the henhouse! But Bum was not in the henhouse! Bum was in the tiny room in the front of the building.

A terrible crashing sound came from the henhouse. Chickens were unmistakably squawking. There was no doubt in my mind now. Bum had somehow gotten into the main part of the henhouse. He was attacking chickens—it couldn't be anything else. Somehow he had forced his way through the tiny door to the chickens.

I could only guess that Bum had lost his mind. Knowing Bum, he'd make fast work of those clumsy birds. In a short time he would kill every one of them. But why? What had happened to him? On other days he never even paid any attention to those dumb birds. He never looked at them— they were beneath him.

I had to face it—it probably would be the end of Bum. How the hell could I explain away twenty-five dead chickens! We couldn't even give him away! My dad would just shoot him with that old Springfield rifle that Uncle Henry had brought home.

I got out of bed; I had to do something. I could never get back to sleep anyway. I put on my robe and slippers, but I certainly was in no hurry. I knew what the outcome was going to be. I was going to be defeated and so was Bum.

Slowly I walked down the stairs. It was time to surrender; there could be no defense. The biggest lie in the world could not help Bum now.

The kitchen light was on! "Oh no," I said out loud. "Dad's already come down. He's at the henhouse now. Wait 'til he counts those dead chickens! He may even shoot Bum tonight."

The back yard was quiet now. Bum had finished his deadly mission. No more squawking. No more racing around the henhouse. It seemed amazing—there was dead silence.

I didn't want to go into the henhouse. I just stood in the yard. I didn't want to see those dead birds. I didn't want to see my dog shot. I didn't want to see anything. I stood in the ray of light that came from the kitchen window.

My mind was clearing and I finally had some peace. I did not want another dog after Bum. Too many memories. Besides, it wouldn't be fair to another dog. The newcomer would never measure up.

Three minutes later my father came out of the henhouse. He didn't shout or scream at me. What did it mean?

"It looks like Bum has earned his keep this month," he said.

"What do you mean?"

"Go in there and look for yourself. You'll understand what I mean."

"I don't understand," I said.

"Go on in there. Go inside and then you'll understand everything."

The light was on in the henhouse and I slowly pushed the door open. I walked in, but only a few feet. The air was cloudy. It was filled with falling dirt, dust and feathers. It almost choked me.

To my right I could see two chickens perched on an overhead rafter. Then I saw two more and two more. To my left I saw ten, maybe twelve, birds perched on the other side of the room.

The dust was settling now and I could see there were no dead chickens on the floor. It wasn't possible! But there I could see for myself—not a one!

Very slowly I walked the length of the room. I could see Bum now. He was at the very end of the room. His tongue hung from his mouth, and he panted as if he had just finished a long race. As I approached him, his tail began to wag, slowly at first, now faster and faster.

On the floor lay the final answer to the entire affair. Next to Bum's paws lay a red fox.

I touched the fox and stroked its coat slowly. His color was almost pure orange. His tail was long and very thick. Strangely, the bottoms of his legs and feet looked as if they had been dipped in black paint. His nose was shiny black and very small. His tiny white teeth protruded from his mouth. He was beautiful.

Bum would be spared. He had gone from villain to hero. Thank God for mini-miracles.

The actual contest had been a short one, but the chase had not been so short. The fox was fast and cunning. Bum must've chased him around the henhouse ten times before he caught him. Those poor chickens must've felt the end of the world was coming, and for them it almost had.

"Good boy, Bum," I said, stroking his neck and shoulder. "Good boy." He knew what I meant and he was satisfied.

In the morning I'd take that fox over to Will. The pelt was perfect. Will would skin him out. The fox might even bring as much as one dollar. Of course, I'd have to split it with Will, but that was all right—I could use the fifty cents.

"Good boy, Bum. Good boy." I stroked his neck again and again. He was satisfied.

The legend of Bum was growing.

Chapter V

Johnny McCann's dad owned an auto repair garage. It really wasn't much of a garage, but it was a good little business. The building was simply the double garage next to their house and Mr. McCann used it for anything that pertained to auto repair. He worked on tire changes, engine overhauling, transmission repair, paint jobs, and everything in between.

John's father never finished the sixth grade—no training in auto mechanics. He was completely self-taught, yet was probably the best at his trade in Lawrence County.

His dad was a disciplinarian with Johnny and his older brothers. If supper was at 6:00 P.M., the four boys were to be home five minutes before six o'clock. They were good students in school and they were in church every Sunday morning.

If Mr. McCann told you the repair was thirty-five dollars before the work began, that's exactly what it was after the work was done. I can't remember hearing anyone ever criticize him or his work. The old fella had left his mark on his sons, and that probably was the biggest reason everyone in our gang liked Johnny so much.

It was Saturday morning and of course, there was no school. I had absolutely nothing to do, so Bum and I meandered over to McCann's Garage.

Outside the garage lay Buster, their old beagle. In his earlier days, Buster had been an outstanding rabbit dog, and Mr. McCann and his older sons had shot many cottontails over him. But Buster was fifteen now and his hunting days were about over. Bum liked Buster and they sniffed noses as we arrived at the garage that morning.

Johnny had seen us from a window in the house and came outside. The two of us talked but mostly watched his father work on an old Buick. From time to time Johnny's oldest brother worked with his father, but today Mr. McCann worked alone. Johnny and I had no idea what work was being done, but we watched intently. His father worked steadily and never said a word to us. He probably didn't want us in the garage, but he never said a word until this day. And when he spoke to me, it was a disturbing scene.

He wiped both his hands vigorously on a red cotton rag and walked toward Bum and me. He didn't speak until he stood directly before us. He looked different and a bit intimidating.

"Jim," he said, looking directly at me, "the last five or six times you've come here I've had tools come up missing. I have kept an inventory and I'm positive of what I say."

"But sir, I . . ."

"Now, you don't need to say anything, I'm certain about what I said. I checked the tools in the morning and they were there. At the end of the day they were gone. It only happened on those days you came over!"

I looked at Johnny. His head was down and he looked at the floor of the old garage. He was deeply wounded, probably even more than I was.

"Now, Jimmy, you go on home and take your dog. I can't afford to lose any more tools, so I don't want you to come back. Now you go on home and take Bum with you."

Hurt and still not certain what he was talking about, I started for home. I called to Bum several times, but I never remember him coming to me. It didn't matter; he knew the way home and I kept walking.

•   •   •

The following morning was terrible. A dull sick feeling filled my stomach. I was not physically sick, but I felt awful. The thought of anyone thinking I was a thief was unbearable. I liked Mr. McCann, and I couldn't live with the thought of him thinking I stole from him. I was also very frightened that he would forbid Johnny to stay in our group.

I tied Bum near the henhouse. He didn't seem to mind the chain; he seemed like he was tired and appreciated the little nap. I returned to the house and walked around with nothing to do but be a companion to my misery.

The doorbell rang and I walked slowly to the front door. I slowed my walk even more as I began to reach the door, for I did not want to be greeted with the possibility of any more grief.

Incredibly, it was Johnny! Quickly I opened the door—he might have had some good news!

"John, come inside," I said.

"No, you come outside."

"What's wrong? Why don't you want to come inside? We can talk in here."

"I don't want anyone to hear us."

Outside we sat on the cement front steps. My mind raced with anxiety, but I worked hard not to speak. I hoped Johnny had good news and didn't wish to keep him from talking.

"Jim, I've been thinkin' about this a lot."

"Thinkin' about what?"

"About this tool business."

"What about it?"

"Each time you've come over, there has only been you, me, and my dad at the garage, along with Bum and Buster."

"Okay."

"Well, I didn't take those tools. I know you didn't take those tools, and I know my dad didn't misplace those tools. I know his record of the tools is accurate."

"Okay, what's next?"

"You promise not to laugh at me?"

"Okay, I promise. Now what is it?"

"It has to be Bum or Buster."

"Oh John, that's the dumbest-ass thing I ever heard. Bum stealin' tools? Buster stealin' tools? What's the matter with you? You crazy?"

"You promised not to laugh at me!"

"I'm not laughin' at you, John, but that's ridiculous! Really, it is!"

"No it isn't! Oftentimes dogs bury their food the way squirrels do. Other animals do that too!"

"I know that! But this isn't food!"

"Lots of times dogs hide their toys and other things like that."

He kept talking, but I wasn't listening. Johnny was a smart guy – everyone knew that, but this time he was living on another planet.

"Jim, I've got a plan. Do you wanna hear it?"

"Okay, John, what's your plan," I asked disgustedly. I really couldn't have cared less, but I pretended I wanted to hear it.

"My dad has to deliver a car tonight in New Wilmington at five o'clock. That means he'll be leavin' the garage at four-thirty. He won't be back until around five-thirty. That'll give us plenty of time to test my plan."

"And what is your plan?" I asked, very disgustedly.

"We'll lay five or six tools out in the open so the dogs can't help but see them. Then we'll just disappear. We'll watch these tools from a distance and see if the dogs pay any attention to them. If they take any of them, then we'll quietly follow them. What do you think?"

"Oh, it's a great plan, John, just great!" I said, more disgusted than ever.

"Good," he said. "Just don't forget to be there at four-thirty—better yet, be there a few minutes after four-thirty." I nodded, not even bothering to speak. Of course the whole thing was a joke; Johnny had flipped his noodle. But what else could I do? I had no other plan.

A little after 4:30 P.M., Bum and I headed over to Johnny's. We walked slowly; I wanted to be absolutely certain I didn't arrive before his dad had left. I still felt the plan was nuts, but it was the only hope I had.

Johnny was waiting at the entrance to the garage. He nodded toward the garage for me to see what he had done. He had placed a small table at the right side of the doorway. Tools were on the table in very plain view—a rubber hammer, two screwdrivers, three wrenches, and two pairs of pliers.

We eased back slowly into the grapevine in John's back yard. The vine was thick with grapes and covered us easily. Both dogs were in the garage and had no idea where we had gone. We did not move and even breathed quietly. For nearly five minutes nothing happened.

Then Bum came to the entrance of the old garage and lifted his leg. After this he stood motionless, except for his head. He moved his head slowly to the right and then slowly to his left. He was very cautious—almost sneaky.

Then Buster came to the entrance. He also began to survey the yard in a very suspicious manner. They stood there like two sentries guarding some military installation. Johnny and I never moved. We breathed so softly we could hear our hearts beating.

At last, Bum broke ranks. He walked to the tiny table and securely took a screwdriver in his mouth. At that moment, Buster broke ranks and started toward the house. Bum followed him—two soldiers marching smartly to some military objective.

"That damn Bum," I said to myself. "That dirty sneaky guy." Johnny had been right about everything. "Damn!" Why did I ever question him? He always was the smartest guy I ever knew.

I started to leave the cover of the old grapevine, but Johnny stopped me with his right hand. He shook his head sideways and I understood.

"No," he whispered, "don't show yourself! We want to see where they go. We may find those other tools. We want those other tools most of all."

We stayed behind the vine. Both dogs moved to the back porch. They never hesitated, but went into an opening next to the steps and down under the porch. Buster led the way and Bum followed. Now we knew!

We hurried from the vine to the back porch. We didn't want to give any time for either dog to leave their little hideout. Most of all, we wanted to find all the tools, especially those ones taken previously.

"Bum, come here," I commanded.

He came out of his secret underground hideout with a very casual look on his face, as if he were saying, "Oh, hi, it's so nice to see you." But he didn't fool me. The sneaky guy had been caught in the act. A moment later Johnny called Buster. He quickly came out and did not play the innocent role. He was guilty! His head was down and his droopy Beagle ears almost touched the ground.

Johnny crawled into the little space between the steps and the porch. The entrance was small, but he made it. A minute later he emerged with a huge smile on his face. He held up seven other tools that had been taken on other days. The tools had a light film of rust on them, but it could easily be removed.

"Be sure to come over tonight after supper. I want my dad to see these tools. I'll clean this rust off with a little oil and some steel wool. Don't forget."

"I won't forget," I said.

Bum and I went home. Strangely, I felt no anger or bitterness toward him. He had caused me much grief, but of course he didn't understand all that.

I looked down at him and he looked back at me. Everything was good again, everything was the same, yet not exactly the same. I understood that he was even smarter than I had thought he was. There was a cleverness about him, a wisdom that I was just beginning to understand.

•   •   •

That night Bum and I returned to the McCanns' garage. Johnny and his dad were actually waiting for us.

"Johnny told me the whole story, Jim," said Mr. McCann. "That's a smart Airedale you have, but I'd like to make a suggestion. When you come back, and we want you to come back, it would probably be a good idea to have Bum on a leash. It might solve a few problems."

"Thanks, Mr. McCann. Thanks."

On our way home I felt wonderful—absolutely wonderful. I'd never felt any better. I wanted Johnny and his dad to like me. I guess I needed them to like me, and I had been completely vindicated.

He had said, "When you come back, and we want you to come back." How good that sounded! How sweet it was.

Chapter VI

There were few experiences in life more enjoyable than fishing in the Neshannock Creek at night. July and August were warm and pleasant in the evenings. During the daytime these months were hot, but nights were different. We slept right on the beach.

On the beach at night we had only two small enemies: the tiny stones under our mattresses, and the mosquitoes.

The stars were everywhere, bright and clear. I never knew much about astronomy, but Johnny and Will did. They knew all the constellations. They knew the different stars were at different places at different times of the year. I knew none of it, so I kept quiet and hoped to learn something.

We would spread our blankets and sleeping bags over the tiny pebbles to cushion the beach. We never got in the sleeping bags or under the blankets. But we were glad we had them, and used them only as mattresses.

Johnny always built a fire. It kept away most of the mosquitoes—but not all. The fire always left a strange odor on us. We smelled a little like hickory-smoked food, but at least it kept bugs away. We swam in the buff and came back to the fire to dry off after the swim.

We fished with our rods off and on all night. We'd fish a little, go to sleep, then wake up and fish again. We'd put more wood on the fire, catch a few trout and go back to sleep again. We'd wake up and the routine would begin again. Usually at least one of us was awake at different times during the night.

Shortly after dawn Will would clean the fish and Johnny would use the fire to cook. We put large rocks around our little fire on which the skillet would rest.

Johnny was a good cook and made a great breakfast. He would bring potatoes and bread in a sealed container from home. Charlie would bring milk in half-pint bottles and leave them in the creek to keep cool all night.

Pan-fried trout fillets, home-fried potatoes, bread, and milk for breakfast. We ate right on the beach. It was wonderful.

Oftentimes I helped Johnny with breakfast. One morning while cutting potatoes, I noticed Johnny's head.

"John, the scalp of your head is brown! Did you know that?"

"Jim, what's the matter with you? Man, I'm brown all over."

He was, too! He was brown all over and none of us had even noticed it. Forty years later the country was tearing itself apart over race and color, but we never noticed.

We lived in another time, a secluded world, almost another planet. We lived in a world of unspoiled forests, creeks, and rivers. We lived in a world of dogs, fishing, swimming, girls, and sleeping on the beach. We knew our neighbors and cared about our neighborhood. We were very happy in this world and did all we could to enjoy it to the fullest.

That night the five of us fished, counted the stars, and slept on the beach at the Neshannock. We were all there, Rome, Charlie, Will, Johnny, me, and of course, Bum. Bum lay on his stomach in a few inches of water in a small cove. It was cool for him and as usual, his eyes were only half closed. It almost seemed that he never slept, even at night. He was always afraid he would miss something.

Suddenly the creek came alive. There was thrashing in the water in the middle of the Neshannock. Up out of the water came a beautiful rainbow. Charlie had hooked a good one. But we knew you never count your fish until they are in the net. Charlie knew he had a good one and held the rod high. Steadily he pulled in the floating line with one hand and cranked the reel on his fly rod with the other.

The rainbow jumped again, totally out of the water. His line then raced up current and then changed direction down the current. We stood at the edge of the water about thirty feet away watching the drama. Bum came from the shallow cove and stood next to us. He wanted a piece of the action.

Charlie at last worked the trout into the shallow water. The big fellow was very tired now and the contest was ending.

Bum rushed forward. In this shallow water he could easily grab that trout and that's what he wanted to do. But Charlie knew Bum's tricks and he held the rainbow high in the net.

Later we measured him at twenty-six inches. The largest and most beautiful Rainbow we would ever see was only a few feet away from him now.

The debate immediately began whether to keep him or not. Charlie was quiet, perhaps feeling a little guilty about his success. He remained neutral.

Will wanted to return him to the creek. He hoped to see more fish like him next year and in the future. Johnny wanted him for breakfast. They debated. Charlie and I listened and would not vote. In the end Rome broke the tie. The vote went with Johnny and breakfast.

We still had to be careful with the fish; only a few feet away Bum watched quietly. It was easy to understand that he would lunge at his first good chance. He had a powerful curiosity for fur, fish, and fowl.

Suddenly Bum returned to the creek. He raced through the shallow water toward the middle of the stream. Now he began to swim toward the other side of the Creek.

"Jim, there's a coon on the other side," whispered Will. "I can just barely make him out at the water's edge. That's where Bum's headin'."

"I don't see nothin'," snapped Charlie.

"I do," said Will. "There's just enough moonlight and Bum's gonna be there in about fifteen seconds."

"You're right, Will," said Johnny. "I can see him now. And that coon's playin' in the shallows."

We could all see him now! He moved slowly. He was a large raccoon, probably a big old male.

"We oughta have some real action in about four or five seconds," said Will, his voice showing the excitement we all felt. "There they go."

At the very last instance the big coon saw Bum, but it was too late. Bum crashed into him! Above the sound of the rushing water we could hear them. Bum growled and the raccoon made that strange chattering sound.

"We oughta get over there," snapped Charlie. "I'd like to see this up close. This is gonna be good."

"No way," said Will emphatically. "You git over there and you may git the hell bit out of you by both animals. Stay here! Besides, Bum knows what he's doin'."

The two animals thrashed in the shallow water. Bum was still growling but the coon was now silent. Something very old and primitive was unfolding in front of us. The wildness of the coon and the fierceness of the wolf were locked in deadly combat. Nothing would stop them now. It would be a struggle to the end.

Suddenly the coon was loose! He had slipped from Bum's grip, and Bum seemed confused. He looked around for the animal. Strangely, the coon was now swimming toward the middle of the creek. The middle was the deepest, probably four or five feet deep.

"What the hell's goin' on?" shouted Charlie

"Jim, this is serious," barked Will. "This is damn serious! Once they get to the deep water in the middle, it could be over."

"What the hell are you talking about," I growled. "Bum can handle any raccoon, regardless how big."

"No, he can't!"

"The hell he can't."

"Jim, I'm tellin' ya, you're wrong!" shouted Will. "On land, yes, but that coon will drown Bum in the deeper water. That's why he's headin' for the middle! They get on a dog's head and try to hold it under. My dad's told me that many times. This is bad, Jim, real bad!"

Will was right. Both animals were now in the middle of the creek. The coon worked himself to the side of Bum's head and neck. With his tiny claws he grabbed Bum's hair and pulled himself onto Bum's head.

Bum went under. The old coon had fought dogs before. He was a wily old devil. We were watching my dog drown before us.

"Help me!" I screamed. "Help me! Come on, let's cross. We can make it."

It was slow going in the current. We tried to go faster, but we were afraid of falling. I led the group. Charlie was last, having put his fish on the bank near our rods.

We reached the middle. The water almost reached our shoulders. Walking was impossible and the four of us began to swim. It was rough going, but we worked hard at it.

By the time we reached the middle, both animals were gone. Perhaps both of them had drowned and had been swept downstream. The current was strong and there was no telling where Bum was now.

My heart would surely burst. The swimming had tired me, but most of all I could do nothing for my dog. Inwardly I screamed, I bled, and I was terrified. My dog had drowned before my eyes. It was over.

"There he is!" yelled Johnny.

For an instant I was saved, but only for an instant. On the far shore the raccoon was almost to the water's edge. He had made it and would soon be heading inland to safety.

And then what seemed to be a miracle happened. Bum was chasing the coon up the beach. Where he had been, how he had got there and how he had gotten back, we never knew.

The coon saw him and started back to the creek. Again the smaller animal sought the safety of the deep water. This time there would be no reprieve and no contest. Bum met him about ten feet from the water's edge and struck him viciously. His upper lip rose and we could see his entire upper white fang. He held the coon by the throat while growling steadily. It was a short contest. The anger, frustration, and pain from the first struggle showed as he held the animal. It appeared the coon was dead, but Bum held on.

At last we reached the far bank. We stood exactly where the water touched the stones of the beach. No one spoke. We continued to watch. Bum continued to hold. No longer did he growl, but he would not let go. We wanted to move closer and see the coon, but did not go forward. Bum continued to hold his fallen opponent.

Bum continued to hold him. After what seemed like hours I finally spoke to him. "Good boy, Bum. Good boy."

The coon was even larger than we thought, the largest we'd ever seen. At last it now appeared that Bum might let go of his trophy.

I did not reach for the coon. Bum's blood was up and I did not try to take the animal from him. I was taking no chances. I petted his head as I spoke to him.

My four friends had stood and watched silently. No one had said a single word since Johnny had yelled that he had seen the raccoon. Now they spoke.

"Wait til I get to school," said Johnny. "The kids'll never believe it. They'll never believe me! You guys gotta back me up when I tell it, otherwise they'll think I'm lyin'. You gotta back me up."

"We will," said Charlie. "We'll back you up—don't worry about it."

"I'll back you up, too," said Rome.

"Jim, you pick up the coon," said Will. "He might not like it if I touched it. He'll probably let you get 'im.""

We guessed that the coon weighed about thirty pounds. We all examined it closely, and Bum didn't seem to care at all. He was very tired now and I wondered if he could get back across the creek.

"Jim, that hide is a good one," said Will. "It's not torn up at all and we oughta make some money on it."

"Good," I said.

"I'll skin him in the morning. I don't wanna do it now; Bum might wake up and get excited again. I'll do it in the morning, though. He's way too heavy to carry home like this."

For nearly half an hour we sat in silence on the far side of the creek. The sound of the rushing water was the only sound we could hear. All our sleeping things were on the far side of the creek. We knew we had to go back, but no one wanted to take that first step into that cold water.

We had no trouble falling asleep that night. Will turned down the wick on the old Pennsylvania Railroad lantern to save kerosene. Bum slept on the far left next to his trophy. It was the only night he didn't sleep in the shallow inlet.

• • •

The next day Dad and I took Bum to the vet. There was no blood on him; it probably washed off in the Neshannock. But there was some battle damage. Bum had a hole in his left ear. It wasn't huge—about half the size of a dime, but you could look right through that hole and you could see light coming through it. The vet said that he had never seen anything quite like it.

Bum also had a straight-line cut on his left shoulder. It was about three inches long and looked as if it had been hit with a straight razor. I swear a surgeon with a small scalpel couldn't have made a neater incision.

"What do you think about that wound on his shoulder, Doctor?" asked my dad. "Do you think it could use a couple of small stitches?"

"Has the dog been inoculated for rabies?"

"Yes," said Dad.

"I wouldn't worry about it then."

"You wouldn't worry about it? Are you sure that thing will heal? It's three or four inches long. It's a nasty looking thing."

"He'll be okay. In a day or two there'll be huge scabs on the ear and shoulder. They'll be pretty thick scabs, so keep an eye on them. Don't pick at them. Just leave them alone. If there's a problem, just gimme a call. They'll both heal and he's a pretty tough guy."

A year later in the spring, when we cut Bum's winter coat, you could see that straight-line scar on his shoulder. He carried it all his life. The hole in his ear also filled nicely.

The vet was right on both counts. The big scabs eventually fell off both wounds, and Bum was a pretty tough guy.

When Johnny got back to school he told the story again and again. We all backed up his exciting version of the contest. In fact, we all told the story.

Will and I split the seventy-five cents we got for the coon's pelt. It became part of a beautiful full-length coat. Bum's reputation was growing and growing.

Chapter VII

It was time for our annual trek up the Shenango River. The Shenango actually flowed much closer to our homes than the Neshannock, but of course, we liked the trout from the creek. Along with the trout, the Neshannock had some rock bass, bluegills, and a few largemouth bass. The Shenango also had some rock bass, bluegills, and largemouth. No trout. The Shenango also had big carp, huge catfish, and muskellunge.

We fished the Shenango in the early morning. It wasn't far from home and everyone was ready to fish. It was a good day. We had our poles this day instead of the fly rods used at the creek.

Johnny and Rome fished for bass. They used nightcrawlers and soft shelled crabs, whichever bait drew the attention of the lunker largemouth. On the bank of the river, fifty feet downstream, Charlie and I set our sinkers to keep the bait near the bottom. We wanted to catch a huge blue channel catfish. A short distance away, Will hooked a six-inch chub on his line. He was after muskies. They were hard to catch and even harder to land. Fishermen should be quiet and patient for muskies and Will was both.

Unlike the creek, the Shenango flowed slowly and quietly. The smooth flow of the river oftentimes hid its depth. In some spots it was ten to fifteen feet deep.

The five of us settled in quietly. Will, Rome, Johnny, Charlie, and I watched our lines as the Shenango steadily moved along. Bum sat nearby. Our lines, heavy with lead sinkers, held fast in the river.

Bum watched our fishing lines carefully. There were no little coves or inlets of shallow water in the Shenango in which he could lie. Only when one of us moved did his eyes leave the river.

A small noise directly behind us in the bushes got our attention. Bum heard it also and immediately left us, crashed into the brush, and investigated everything nearby.

Ten seconds later a large fox squirrel noisily climbed a shag-bark hickory tree. From a safe branch above, the squirrel defiantly chattered at Bum for bothering him. Bum came out from the brush, looked at the squirrel above, barked at him, and then quietly took his original place on the cool dirt bank near us.

Since we came to the river so infrequently, it held much fascination for us. It was strange—even a little mysterious. Unlike the Neshannock, it was never cold, almost warm. It was not quick moving or noisy, but slow, quiet—even lazy. A canoe or small boat could be used nicely to hunt on this river. It would be a great spot for a quiet duck hunter.

"Got him!" yelled Rome from downstream.

"What is it?" asked Charlie.

"Largemouth, I think," answered Rome.

"Is he a keeper?" I asked.

"We'll know in about a minute," answered Rome.

Bum rose to his feet. He'd been on many fishing trips and knew what was happening. However, he did not jump into this unfamiliar river, but stood firmly on the river's edge.

"I think he's kinda small," said Johnny. "Your pole isn't bent very much. He's gotta be on the small side."

The bass fought bravely and broke the surface of the river. Whatever size he was, he was making a good fight of it.

"You were right, John," said Rome. "He's a little small and I'm gonna throw 'im back."

Rome quickly removed the hook from the bass and held him up for all to see.

"How big would you guess?" asked Charlie. "Is he twelve inches?"

"No," said Rome. "He's eight, maybe nine inches—no more. He's definitely goin' back."

Bum barked at Rome. He wanted to see the little fish more closely.

"No, Bum, you can't have 'im! He's too small!" Rome dropped it into the river and it quickly darted away.

Quiet returned to the river bank, but not for very long. A few minutes later the action started again.

"I got one," yelled Johnny excitedly. "And I think this guy is definitely a keeper, I'm sure of it. This guy can fight."

"You always say that," snapped Charlie. "Let's see 'im after he's caught, if you can land 'im."

"I'll land 'im—wait and see! Look at my pole. You still think I got a small one on my line? Look at that pole! You wouldn't wanna bet on this fish, would ya, Charlie?"

Charlie said nothing. He could see Johnny's pole and realized that no small fish could bend it like that.

"Well, maybe I'm wrong about this one," said Charlie. "I'd still like to see 'im before I say anything more."

The fish, probably another bass, thrashed on the surface. Johnny kept his pole high. He had the fish under control.

Bum started to bark. He thought every fish caught should be personally inspected by him and we usually obliged him.

"I think you were wrong about this fish, Charlie," I said. "This guy is bigger than you thought and this is turnin' into a good show."

Johnny held his pole high but made little headway with the fish. He let out some line, hoping to tire the fish, but the bass swam to Johnny's left, then to his right. The fish broke the surface and dived again.

No one spoke, including Johnny. There was no doubt with anyone that the fish was of good size and a good fighter. But there was growing doubt in everyone's mind, including Johnny's, that the fighting fish would be landed at all.

The tension was growing, and it was very noticeable on Johnny's face. No one spoke. No one wanted to jinx our friend.

Bum barked. Then he barked again and again. He was impatient like all of us.

"Bum, hush up," I yelled. He paid no attention to me and barked again. "Bum, shut up!" I yelled. This time he listened to me. Some of the tension seemed to be broken.

Slowly, Johnny was beginning to win the contest. The big fish was tiring and Johnny steadily brought him closer to shore.

Johnny stood in the water about five feet from shore. The water wasn't very deep and Bum plunged in with him; he could contain his own excitement no longer.

Johnny grasped the fish by its lip and held it high, keeping it from Bum. The four of us cheered while Bum barked.

Rome's tape measure showed it was twenty-three inches long—a real beauty. The contest had lasted nearly twenty minutes, but the memories would never leave us. The fish was definitely a keeper and each of us would've been glad to take him home.

Will, having come the farthest to see the fish, said, "Look at how big his mouth is. And will you look at his stomach! His gut is huge! He's been eatin' real good!"

"Here's my stringer," said Rome. "Git 'im on it before he gits loose and flops back in the river."

"John, is that the biggest bass you ever caught?" I asked.

"It's the biggest bass I ever saw," said John. "Smallmouth or largemouth, he's the biggest one I ever saw."

Rome secured the stringer on the bank and the bass stayed in the river. The calm was returning to our group. We were envious of Johnny but happy for our friend.

Bum again lay down on the bank of the river while the five of us quietly returned to watching our lines. The sun rose high in the sky and the temperature was slowly rising. Despite the sun, our spot on the bank was pleasant—almost cool. We fished from the shade under two large cottonwood trees. It was a good place to be, but again the tranquility was not to last.

From my left, Will shouted, "Somebody's line is movin' in the water. Somebody's got a fish on."

"It's mine," said Charlie as he hurried to pick up his pole. "I'm glad you yelled, Will—I was really daydreamin'."

"I got one too," said Rome, excitedly.

"This guy is big," said Charlie. "I can hardly move 'im. I'm afraid he's gonna do whatever he wants."

"Don't horse him in," I warned. "If he's really big, he'll snap your line. You don't know what you got there."

"I know what I got here," said Rome. "This guy's a midget. I'll trade ya fish , Charlie. You can take mine—we'll swap."

"No thank you," said Charlie emphatically. "I'm keepin' him, if I can. What do you think he is, Jim?"

"I think he's a big cat."

"Shovelhead or blue channel?"

"Oh, I got no idea! We're just gonna have to wait till you get him in."

"I know what I got," said Rome, smiling. "Look at that little fart! He's only four inches long!" Rome held him up for all to see. "He is kinda pretty, though—sunfish, I guess."

"Throw him back, Rome," said Johnny. "He's way too small to keep."

"I know he is. I'm gonna throw him back. I just wanna look at him a second. He's pretty. If we didn't have so many worms, I'd cut him up for bait."

From Rome's little sunfish we all turned back to watch Charlie. This was the main event and the outcome was far from over.

The big fish had almost reached the far bank. It seemed Charlie was losing the struggle. He tried to bring him closer but the big fish slowly moved away.

"You gotta git him back, Charlie!" shouted Will. "If he gits any farther from ya, ya prob'ly won't git 'im back! If he is a big cat, he won't tire quickly like a lot of fish."

"I know," said Charlie. "I'm doin my best!" His voice was desperate now. "I know he's too far out, but he won't budge! I don't wanna horse 'im."

The four of us now kept quiet. We knew Charlie was doing his best. His voice showed his concern and we didn't want to make things worse.

But as we grew quiet Bum rose and walked to the water's edge. He saw the line moving in the water and knew what was happening. He began to bark.

"Bum—shut up!" I yelled.

This time he listened to me and stood at the bank watching the action. We wanted nothing more to add to the tension on Charlie. There was silence now. Only the cranking on the reel was heard as Charlie was holding on.

Charlie kept the pole high and very slowly the line came in. He wanted to work the reel faster, but didn't. The fish came closer and closer. For the first time it seemed that Charlie could win this contest.

The big fish was in the middle of the Shenango now. Charlie had gotten him back from the far bank of the river. He breathed heavily and felt the stress from the struggle.

"Man, am I tired," he said. "I can't believe this guy has worn me out so much. He feels like a whale. I'm absolutely exhausted."

"You're doin' all right," I said. "Keep steady on him. You're doin' all right. Another twenty-five feet and you'll have him."

Throughout the entire struggle no one had seen the fish. He had kept himself deep, away from all eyes, deep in the dark bottom of the river. The five of us, and Bum, stood at the water's edge and waited for our first glimpse.

"I see him!" screamed Will. "He's a big catfish—a huge catfish. He must be forty inches. Hold on, Charlie!!"

The huge fish was now on the surface. Now we all saw him. Charlie held on. Will screamed about his size. Johnny and Rome yelled for Charlie to keep cranking. Bum barked. I roared with excitement. Everyone broke loose.

The catfish on the surface began to thrash. He moved to his left, whipped his tail and moved to his right, then back to his left again. He was not tired at all and would not keep still. It was a desperate struggle and he twisted like a small alligator. He fought with determination and would not permit us to get him to the bank.

Then Charlie's line went limp. He was gone. The fish had done what he wanted—he had broken that line. The ten-pound test line could not hold. He was gone.

We all stood silently, including Bum, at the river's edge. There was no need to speak; we had seen it. Charlie had also fought a good fight.

"You did your best, Charlie," said Will. "The line just wouldn't hold. You did all you could. That old guy had probably broken lines before. You did your part; the line lost him."

No one else spoke. Charlie was disappointed and Will had said just enough. We each went to our own poles and returned to the river. It was silent again.

For several minutes Charlie stood at the river's edge. He looked across to the bank on the far side. It was over and he let go of it.

Bum returned to his spot about ten feet from the water's edge. He rested his head on his front paws and half closed his eyes, only half. As always, he didn't want to miss anything.

The Shenango didn't disappoint us. The action started again and we all took notice.

"There's somethin' on my line," whispered Will. "See it movin'? That's definitely a fish – maybe a big one, too."

"Get your pole, Will," I urged. "Grab it and set the hook. Don't let him get away."

"No," said Will. "I'm gonna let him take it real good. I'll set it in a minute. I got fifteen pound test line on that pole, and a steel leader, and I'm ready for that cat this time."

We all watched that line go across the river. Even Bum watched silently.

"Seven, eight, nine, ten," counted Will. Now he yanked the line hard, setting his hook. He had been patient. Now the fun began and Will was ready.

"What bait do you have on there, Will?" I asked.

"I got a six-inch chub on there. Anything that'll take that has got to be a big fella."

"Your bait is bigger than that sunfish I got earlier," said Rome. "I probably shoulda kept him for bait myself."

The fish started across the river just as Charlie's catfish had. But then he suddenly started downstream, using the current to his advantage. Will quickly raised the pole and reeled hard. He was not going to let this fish get far from him.

"Do you think he's another catfish?" asked Charlie. "He's runnin' a little bit like mine did. I wonder if he's the same fish."

"I don't know what he is," Will said softly. "I can't tell. I know one thing, no little fish coulda taken that chub."

The big fish started back upstream. He didn't exactly move the way Charlie's catfish had. He didn't go across the river but up and down the river.

"What are you tryin' to do with him?" asked Rome. "Are you bringin' him in, or what?"

"I'm doin' nothin' with him! He's goin' wherever he wants. I just hope to tire him out and steadily bring him in. With fifteen-pound test line, I figure I got a little advantage."

"I bet he's a big channel cat," said Johnny. "I'll bet he's just like Charlie's! Maybe he is Charlie's! You just wait and see. This river is full of big catfish."

"Maybe you're right. Right now I'm just hangin' on. I can't do anything with him. You worry about what he is."

Up and down the river he went, then up and down again. He reminded us of a wild horse. Will had a rope around his neck, but he wasn't comin' into that barn.

"I'm getting' damn tired of this!" snapped Will. "My patience is runnin' out fast. I wanted to wear him out, but he ain't wearin'."

"Try trickin' 'im and bringin' 'im in real slow," said Johnny.

"Good idea—I'll try it. I don't wanna be here at seven o'clock tonight. He's just damn hard to move."

Very slowly Will moved him closer to the shore. The movement was slow, but Will was starting to win. The fish was about thirty feet from shore.

The water now was swirling violently. The fish seemed to know Will's plan. He would not come any closer to shore. On the other hand he could not escape, either. He twisted and thrashed in the water but remained at thirty feet away. It was deadlock. Neither side could move the other. Then a strange thing happened.

The big fish slowly let himself rise until he reached the surface. He could see us now and we could see him.

"Will, look at him!" I screamed. "He's a muskie—look at his eyes!"

"I see him," yelled Will. "I never thought he was a catfish. I had a little feeling he was a muskie. I even hoped he was a muskie."

He lay motionless on the surface with a defiant look in his eyes. He lay there like a prehistoric crocodile, more lizard than fish, from another world.

Bum growled menacingly at him. It almost seemed as if Bum knew him from another time. The fish was determined not to be brought to land. Will was more determined to land him.

He thrashed the water now with all his strength. He twisted and fought even more violently than the big catfish had.

"I got to take him now. I can't just wait for him to cut my line with those teeth."

Will reeled hard. The muskie pulled hard, but Will was making headway. The distance was twenty-five feet—now twenty feet. The big fish fought back, but Will had saved his own strength until the right time.

The distance was now fifteen feet—only fifteen feet! Will began to run away from the river, working his reel and pole all the time.

"Help me pull him out, you guys! Help me get him!"

The distance was ten feet! Now it was only five! We crashed into the river, but Will had pulled him onto the bank. We jumped back to the bank to hold him.

On the bank we all reached for him, including Bum. The muskie's teeth flashed menacingly and we avoided them. We held his body. He twisted, but we held. Bum snarled again at him, but he avoided the dangerous front end with the teeth.

Rome brought his stringer and a thick tree branch to insert into the mouth of the muskie. Slowly Rome inserted the stringer through the gill, but carefully avoided those teeth.

We all breathed heavily now, almost exhausted, yet jubilant. We congratulated Will and each other. Johnny brought the measuring tape. The tape was four feet long and the muskie was longer.

We were silent. We saw it, but didn't really believe it. The fish was three or four inches longer than the tape. We shook our heads. The fish was over fifty inches long.

We picked up out poles, packed our gear, carried the fish and started for home. Will carried the muskie and stopped regularly to rest. We carried his pole and tackle box and shared his load.

Near the edge of the woods, Bum started along a tiny trail up a steep hill. His nose was to the ground and he was obviously trailing something.

"Where's he goin'?" asked Will.

"I don't know," I said. "I'm too tired to call him back. Don't worry about him—he'll catch up." We picked up the fish and our gear and started on. We had taken only five or six steps when we heard a loud crashing sound and looked behind us at the tiny hill.

Bum came rolling down the little hill, crashing from end to end through the small bushes. From the top of the hill came a heavy buck deer. He had hit Bum at the top of the hill and sent him rolling down. The buck was in velvet, and from only fifteen feet away his twelve points were clearly visible. Bum was not seriously injured, but he had tracked the wrong animal up the wrong hill.

Johnny began to laugh.

"What's so funny?" I asked.

"Bum rollin' down that hill."

"I don't think it's so funny."

"I think it's funny too," said Rome. "I think it's damn funny. It's one of the funniest things I ever saw!"

"That's the first fight I ever saw Bum lose," said Charlie. He also began to laugh.

They were all laughing now. The more they laughed, the harder their laughter got. I was no longer irritated. It was funny. The thought of Bum rolling down that hill brought a little smirk to my face as well. I didn't laugh out loud, but my four friends continued to howl.

Bum walked slowly with his head down. His tail wasn't between his legs, but it wasn't straight up the way it usually was.

The contest had been very short. What Charlie said was true. It was the first fight Bum had ever lost, and the only one he had ever lost.

Chapter VIII

Sally Berger and I had known each other since first grade. She was nice. She was fun to talk with and had a great sense of humor. She was a good student, probably the smartest in our class. She was a very good swimmer and an even better tennis player.

But Sally Berger was changing and everyone noticed. Her waist was small and her hips were noticeable. Her bosom developed nicely and she was curved in the correct places.

Her hair was blond and shone, I swear it shone even when there was no sunlight on it. Her eyes were big and brown and seemed warm. Everyone noticed her. My mother said Sally was a pretty girl but was really beautiful on the inside.

Yes, Sally had changed. She was the first girl I had completely noticed. She was a girl that you'd never forget, either. A man may be married forty years, yet never forget that Sally Berger he had known.

All my friends at school noticed her. Charlie noticed her, Johnny noticed her, and Rome noticed her the most. He rarely mentioned her, but everyone knew how he felt. When he was around her he always seemed to wear his finest clothes.

Yet at our school dances she rarely danced with anyone. She was rarely asked to dance. It wasn't because she didn't know how to dance—she danced very well. She was simply too intimidating to most young men.

Most guys could never believe she could be interested in them. She was too pretty. She was too smart. She was too talented. Most guys felt she would never look at them. There was no other reason that boys shied away from her. No one would admit these things out loud, but they knew the truth.

But I was determined! I was not going to be intimidated. How did anyone know what she really felt anyway? Maybe she felt the same way about me I felt about her? I would not worry about these things like most guys did.

But the next dance was a month away! It would not be until school started in September. I didn't want to wait that long. I couldn't wait that long!

I walked around the house—twice around the house. Where could I meet her? Where could I even see her? I wracked my little brain. There had to be a place where I could meet her.

The third time around the house Bum joined me. He walked with his head down as if he were thinking and trying to help me with my problem. But I couldn't come up with a single idea of where I could meet her.

"Jimmy," called my mother from inside the house. "Come in here—I need you."

"Where are you?"

"I'm in the kitchen. I am making apple pies. I need you to peel some of these apples. And tie up Bum at the henhouse."

I washed my hands at the kitchen sink and made myself ready to work. Yet as I looked at the apples, I could only think of my plans regarding Sally.

"Did you tie up Bum at the henhouse?"

"Oh no, I forgot. I'll go do it now."

"Never mind tying him—just start on these apples. You're getting very lazy about tying him. When you're not with him, you should always have him tied."

"I'm not lazy about tying him—I just forget! I got a lotta things on my mind—really I do."

"You seem to have a lot of things on your mind most of the time. If you do things immediately, there's much less chance of forgetting them. That's a good habit to learn."

She kept talking and I could hear her, but I didn't listen any more. All I could think about was some plan, any kind of plan about seeing Sally. I worked on the apples but could only think about that plan. I had to be careful, for the knife was like a razor. I didn't want some nasty cut, yet couldn't stop thinking about the plan instead of apples.

What was that my mother had said about doing something immediately? She had said if you do something immediately, there's less chance of forgetting it. Yes! Yes, that's exactly what she said.

But how can I see Sally immediately? I have to do these apples. After the apples, I have supper. But after supper, maybe I could see her. Yes! Yes, I could see her then.

I could pretend I was just taking a walk. I'd just happen to be walking past her house. Maybe she won't be home. Maybe she will be home. Maybe she'll be on the porch. If her brother is around, I'll ask him where she is. If nothing works, I'll ring the doorbell.

Once we get talking, I'll know what to say. Who cares what we talk about! Somehow we'll get on her front porch and things will just begin to happen.

•　•　•

There was nothing I could do to speed up the clock for supper. I wanted to read something, anything, hopefully a good fishing magazine—anything to pass the time faster. The sweet smell of pies in the oven was good but did not help me get my mind off Sally.

What seemed like a year finally passed and supper was over. My mother cleaned our table and my sisters helped her. Hazel washed the dishes and Allison dried them and put them in the kitchen cupboard.

After feeding Bum I quietly slipped away from the house. I certainly didn't want to arrive early on Queen's Avenue, so I walked slowly. I had to time the arrival just right. Sally was probably helping her mother after supper and I wanted to give them a little time before my arrival.

The sun looked like a giant golden coin, half of it below the horizon with the upper half above it giving light and warmth. It couldn't be down for another hour. It gave me plenty of time to find her house.

Slowly I walked down Queen's Avenue. Her house could not be far ahead–maybe only three or four houses. There it was—227 Queen's Avenue!

There was a person on her porch. I couldn't see who it was. The closer I got the more it looked like her mother. Yes, it was her mother. No, it was Sally! It was definitely Sally!

What a break! She was on the porch swing, looking down reading something. She had to have a magazine or newspaper. I knew she didn't see me and I had to say something to get her attention.

"Hi, Sally. Is this your house?"

She turned to her left and looked at me on the sidewalk. A nice smile came to her face. "Hi, Jimmy. What are you doing here?"

"I was just takin' a little walk. I didn't know you lived on this street. I was just ready to turn around and head for home."

"Would you like to come up here on the porch? This is a nice swing."

"I guess I could come up for a couple of minutes."

I walked up her small driveway and had the strange feeling she knew I was lying about everything, but I didn't care. What a break finding her here on the porch by herself. And she even asked me to come up! How lucky could I get?

Up the three porch steps and I was on the porch with her. Her hair shone in the fading light as it always did.

"Would you like to sit here on the swing with me?"

"It's a small swing," I said. "Are you sure it's big enough?"

"Oh sure it is. I can just move over a little," she said as her brown eyes flashed at me.

We rocked slowly on the swing and for several minutes we said nothing. I could have sat there for hours. I had no idea what to talk about, so I never said a word. We kept rocking on the swing.

"My brother is at his baseball game."

"When will he be home?"

"Probably in about an hour. Maybe a little longer."

"Good."

"What do you mean?"

"I—I mean it's good he's on a team and he gets to play with his friends. It should be a lot of fun."

"Yes, he seems to like it a lot."

My left hand was on the seat of the swing. She had her right hand on the seat also. The little finger from her hand brushed my hand. I moved my hand a few inches and put it on top of hers. She did not move her hand. It was a good sign and we rocked slowly. We talked about school starting next month. We talked about swimming and tennis. We talked on about everything. We must've talked about twenty minutes, but I could remember very little. All I could think about was moving closer to her and kissing her.

She kept talking and I simply listened. She mentioned both her brothers, and I had forgotten that she had two brothers. One was a sophomore and one a senior at Union High. She continued to talk, but I interrupted her.

Her lips were soft and friendly, and as I kissed her, she kissed me back. I was surprised at my boldness. I didn't put my arm around her but kissed her a second time. It was even nicer than the first time.

I was kissing Sally Berger and holding her hand! No one in the gang would believe it. I wouldn't tell them—they'd never believe me anyway. I wouldn't tell anyone; everyone would know and see soon enough. I was the man! This made me the man! Sally Berger and me. Fourteen years old and I was the man!

I held her hand as she kept talking. I knew I would kiss her again in a few minutes, but right now we would just rock slowly. Then everything began to unravel.

"What is that in our yard?" she asked.

"What is what?"

"What is *that*!" she said, pointing her finger at the front yard. "It looks like the head of an animal! It is an animal. It's a dog or a cat or something."

"Where?"

"Right there, directly in the center of our yard," she said, again pointing at the yard. "It's a dog and it's digging a hole. Don't you see it?"

"I see it now."

"That crazy dog has dug a huge hole and he's in it. Only his head is looking out above the hole."

"I see it clearly now."

"That's your dog. That's your Airedale! This is crazy; what is he even doing here?"

"Oh no, that can't be my dog! My dog's at home. That can't be my dog—I tied him up after supper."

I was lying my tail off and I think she knew it. I had to say something—anything, to try to save my little romance. How the hell could I get out of this? Bum must've followed me from home.

"My dad will be furious. I'm going to get a rake and shovel and fill that hole. I've got to clean up that yard."

"It's not my dog, but I'll fill it in. Get me the rake and shovel and I'll do it."

"No! Go on–leave! I'll take care of it."

"I'll do it," I said. "I can do it."

"No! Just leave! Just leave!" she said, still talking as she entered the garage through the side door. I could still hear her voice from inside the garage.

I looked back to the yard. It was Bum, alright, no doubt about it. He was humped over in the yard and was leaving her a huge pile to shovel into that hole. I didn't know whether she had seen it or not, but it was awful.

Down the three front porch steps I went in one jump. I walked briskly down the driveway. I was destroyed, but there was no point in running, so I slowed to a walk. "Oh no," I said out loud. "This really isn't happening. It can't be happening."

I didn't even look at Bum. I just started up Queen's Avenue. Soon he joined me, though I never called to him.

I'll never know what he was thinking when he followed me. Maybe he was angry or spiteful at being left at home. Maybe he was just digging the way all terriers do. If I had tied him, there would've been no problem for me.

But what would Sally do? That was really all that mattered now. There was no point in staying angry with Bum; his bit part was history now. But what about Sally? Would our little romance overcome this goofy affair? I hoped so. I certainly hoped so.

Chapter IX

Bum loped along casually and I ran hard to keep up with him. We were late for supper and I didn't want to be any later. After leaving Rome's house, we cut through the back alleys trying to shorten the route to Moore Avenue. We cut the corner of the lawn on Harlan's place. It only saved a few seconds as we ran, but since we were already late, every few seconds helped.

"Get off my grass!" someone shouted at me. "Get off my grass and keep off!"

Bum and I stopped. It was Old Man Harlan. I had heard much about him over the years; however I had never actually seen him before.

"I'm sorry we ran over your grass. We only made a couple of footsteps on it and won't do it again."

"I don't care if it was only a couple of footsteps, and I don't care to hear your stupid apology. If you and that dog are on my grass again, I'll shoot that mangy dog."

"Oh shut up, you old fool! That's a terrible thing to say and I'm not paying any attention to you."

"I'm gonna tell your father what you called me. Yes, I am certainly gonna tell him."

"You be sure to tell him. And I'll tell him what you said about shooting my dog."

Bum and I started for home again. I didn't want to hear anything more from that old man.

"You heard what I said! You heard me!"

He kept yelling as Bum and I kept running. The more we ran the more angry I became. It was simply unreal for anyone to even think about shooting a dog for a few steps on their grass. Now I understood why so many people disliked this man.

I could see the house ahead. We slowed to a walk just before I entered the house. I wanted to settle myself. I had to stop thinking about Old Man Harlan and let go of this anger. More than anything, I worried that he would actually do it.

After supper I felt somewhat better, but not completely. Hazel, Allison, and Mother stayed in the kitchen. Dad went to the backyard and trimmed a small blue spruce. I followed him outside and was determined to tell him the entire affair.

He never said a single word as he listened. He worked on the little spruce, but I am sure he heard every word. I had a strange feeling he knew everything even before I said it. I didn't leave out a single thing and pointed out what I had said also. I didn't try to cover up my own behavior.

When I had finished, my father said nothing. For several minutes there was silence as he worked with the tree.

"Jim, I'm sorry you had to go through this sort of thing," he said very slowly. "Paul Harlan has been an angry man for a long time. It's a long story and you probably wouldn't understand it all if I told you, so I won't even go into it. He and his old-maid sister have lived in that rickety house all their lives, first as children and then staying on after their parents died."

"But what if he would shoot Bum?"

My father never directly answered my question, giving me an uneasy feeling that my fears were justified. I listened very carefully to what he would say.

"You're going to have to do what everyone else does—ignore him. Don't go on his street unless it's absolutely necessary! If you have to go on his street, make sure you and Bum are going down the opposite side of the street from his property. It might be a good idea for you never to take Bum over there. Do you understand me?"

"Yes."

"Are you sure you understand me?"

"Yes, I understand!"

Bum and I walked around the backyard. I couldn't get my mind off that old man. Most of all, I couldn't forget that my father had not answered my question. With my luck, the old fool would miss Bum and hit me.

•　　•　　•

The following day Will and I sat on the side steps of the school. It was recess period following lunch. Sally was in the office scheduling a make-up test and was coming later.

The weather outside was wonderful. The trees were yellow, orange, red, brown and green. It was Indian Summer. It was warm, yet pleasant. It was mild, dry and even a little hazy. The leaves crackled under my feet as I walked. It would not last long but was beautiful now.

"Do you know Old Man Harlan?" asked Will.

"What? What did you ask?"

"I asked if you know Old Man Harlan."

It burst out of me like a lake whose dam had been destroyed. The story flowed out of me rapidly. I told Will the whole story, every word, every detail. I told him about my father, our talk, his advice, and everything.

"That does it," said Will.

"Does what?"

"I'm gonna get that old bastard!"

"Why?"

"I've had half a dozen run-ins with that old jerk!"

"What are you gonna do?"

"I'm gonna blow up his outhouse. I'm gonna do it and I'm gonna do it Halloween night!"

"How the hell are you gonna blow up anything? What are you gonna use to blow up somethin'?"

"Dynamite!"

"Where could you get that? Don't be silly! You don't have any dynamite!"

"The hell I don't!"

"You're just talkin' crazy. You're just sayin' anything that comes into your head! Where would you get any dynamite?"

"From my dad and from our garage."

For the first time I realized he would really do it. It was not like Will to talk like this. He was serious and this was not simply idle talk.

"Are you just gonna walk up to your dad and ask for it?" I asked.

"Of course not. I doubt if he even remembers he's got any. He has no idea where he put it."

"Where did he get any dynamite?"

"From Old Man Henderson. They were blowin' up some stumps on Henderson's farm. Farmers get that stuff all the time and they were usin' it just this summer. I just hope it's still good. It's probably okay—it's only a few months old."

"Isn't that stuff dangerous?" I asked.

"A little, but I'll be careful and I know how to use it. I'll be careful with the fuse and match, also."

"Where is it now?"

"You come over tonight as soon as it's dark and I'll show ya. Come to our back porch door."

"Are you sure you're not just jokin'? I don't know whether you're kiddin' me or not."

I knew he was not joking at all. I knew when he talked like this I had better pay attention.

"You be at my back porch door after dark—you'll see it then. You be sure to be there—I need you! And don't bring Bum!"

• • •

I stood in the darkness next to the two rosebushes near Will's back porch. His plan worried me. The use of this dynamite could be very dangerous.

The back door squeaked and I knew it was Will. "Jim, are you out there?" he whispered.

"I'm here."

We headed for the garage. I couldn't see my hand in front of my face, but Will knew where he was going.

"What's that in your hand?" I asked.

"A flashlight."

"Why do you need a flashlight? There's a big overhead light in the garage, isn't there?"

"Yes, but I don't want anyone in the house to see the light on in the garage. If they see it, they're gonna come out and see why it's on. I don't want nobody in that garage but you and me."

In the darkness we moved slowly. In the garage we moved past the car to the back of the building.

"Where is the stuff?" I asked.

"In the old wooden cabinet on the back wall. I saw it just a week ago."

He turned on the flashlight and we followed its beam to the back wall. The beam darted across the wall searching for the little cabinet.

"There it is," said Will.

"It has a padlock on it!"

"I know where the key is."

Will moved his hand along the right side of the cabinet but found nothing. He moved his hand along the left side of the cabinet and again found nothing. He moved his hand along the bottom of the cabinet – no key!

"I thought you said you knew where the key was."

"I do."

"Well, where the hell is it? Did someone move it, or what? We're not getting' in that cabinet without that key!"

Will moved a tiny chair and placed it directly underneath the cabinet. He stood on the chair and slowly moved his hand over the top of the wooden cabinet. Between his fingers, he held the key for me to see.

"I told you I knew where it was."

"You sure as hell took the long way around to find it!"

Will unlocked the padlock and opened the little cabinet door. From the bottom shelf he took two clean cotton rags. Very carefully he took out the long narrow cylinder. The dynamite stick was only an inch thick but about ten inches long. It looked much different than I thought it would.

"There it is," he said. "It's good and dry and as good as ever. That fuse is only about seven or eight inches long, but I'll manage. Ever seen anything like it before?"

"No, never have. That fuse looks awful short. Do you think it's long enough? That little thing worries me. You better really move once it's lit."

"You're right, it's short, but don't worry—I won't stick around. We'll have to run like hell once it starts to burn."

"We? What do ya mean, 'we'? Where do I fit in this? What the hell do ya need me for?"

"Look, didn't that old hermit threaten to shoot your dog? Can you imagine him shootin' Bum? Haven't I had six or seven run-in's with him? Doesn't everyone in Union Township hate that old jackass?"

"Yes, but, but. . .."

"But nothin'! I need you! I need a lookout! You'll stand off hiding about a hundred feet away. If anybody comes by, you come and tell me not to light it. That'll keep anyone from gettin' hurt or killed. After I light it I'll come racin' past you and we'll take off together."

"When's this supposed to happen?"

"This Friday night is Halloween. It's the perfect time. I planned this down to the last detail and it's a perfect plan."

"What time Halloween night?"

"You sneak outa your bedroom window, down the back porch roof the way you always do. Then meet me at that same rose bush near my back porch. Meet me at midnight. Now be there at twelve o'clock sharp! No slip-ups!"

"When will we get the stuff out of the garage?"

"I'll take care of that. I'll have the stuff ready to go. You just be at that rosebush at twelve o'clock sharp. And whatever you do, don't bring Bum! Be certain he's tied!"

"He'll be chained at the hen house."

"When I come runnin' past you, Jim, you better be ready! You better stick to my coattail. Don't wait for nothin'! And keep your back to that outhouse. Don't turn around to look for nothin'! Go straight home and so will I."

"Will, you got any idea what that neighborhood is gonna smell like after we've blown that crap-house? It'll stink for a week!"

"Jimbo, it'll probably stink longer than that! I don't care what it smells like; I don't live next door to him. Besides, he's got it comin'!"

•   •   •

It was past eleven-thirty as I lay in bed. I was fully dressed in bed with a light blanket over me. Mother, Dad, Hazel, and Allison were all in bed. The door to my room was closed as I lay in the darkness.

Strangely, I was very relaxed. I was at peace with everything. Will was right—it was a great plan. All we had to do was to stick to it completely. I was actually envious of him; I wished I had thought of it myself. After the dash home, it would be up the back porch, in through the bedroom window, and off to sleep. It was the perfect alibi. But who would need an alibi? Will was correct again. Everyone in the township hated that old jackass—he would never guess who did it.

My little watch said it was ten minutes to twelve. I must move and I must move quickly! I had to be there at twelve and not be a minute late.

Quietly I slipped out of bed, out the back window and smoothly down the back porch. In twenty seconds I would be at Franklin's rosebush.

Will was waiting. I was two minutes early, but it didn't matter. We were ready. We were like two race horses at the starting gate.

"Have you got the stuff?" I asked.

"Right here," he said, holding it for me to see. "Come on, let's move. We got work to do."

From that moment on we never said a word. We jogged slowly, then walked awhile. Our clothing was dark, and impossible to see, even if anyone was out—which no one was.

We entered the old man's street. The surface of it was brick but we walked quietly. The memory of that day on the street with Bum flashed through my mind. Our resolve was set, nothing would stop us now. Near a small group of trees we stopped and Will pointed at them, indicating for me to hide there. He never said a word and I knew he would be racing back in a few minutes.

I watched him walk away, but lost sight of him very quickly. The darkness and his dark clothing were a perfect camouflage. Into the branches of the little pine tree I stepped. It covered my outline perfectly if anyone were near. Its pine fragrance was sweet and it also would cover any scent I would have.

My eyes never moved. They were rigidly trained on the last place I had seen Will. I could see nothing in the darkness, but I knew when he came he would be exactly where I was watching for him.

There was almost total silence. Only the crickets were my companions. It would not be long now, perhaps a minute, probably less, and he would be racing toward me.

Was that movement? Was the darkness playing games with me? Where was he? He should've been here by now! What the hell was keeping him? Did he have trouble?

There was movement and it was coming toward me. It was Will and he would be at the little pine tree in an instant.

I stepped away from the tree so he would see me. Together we raced across the field; then came the terrific blast behind us. Wind, wood, dirt, debris of all types attacked us from behind, but we kept running.

We never looked back once. We ran hard. We breathed hard and perspired beneath our black sweaters. We ran the entire way to Moore Avenue and never looked back once. We had never said a word since Will had shown me the dynamite.

We reached our yards. Will turned to his left; I turned to my right, heading for the back porch. In less than two minutes I was up the porch and into my dark bedroom.

I removed the dark clothes and laid them on the floor at the end of my bed. I slipped into bed, still breathing heavily after our run. After several minutes my breathing eased. A smile came to my face and I was pleased with our work. Will had been right. It was a great plan. I slept soundly.

•   •   •

Several days later, Will and I walked nonchalantly up the street past the Harlan place. We wanted to evaluate our work. The ground was totally level where the old outhouse had once been. We did not stop along the way, but were very satisfied with our work.

Once again, Will had been right. The neighborhood did not stink for a week. It stunk for a month.

Chapter X

B um could whip every dog in Union Township, except one. A previous contest with that dog had ended in a draw. Neither dog seemed very happy about it and I guess what would happen next was simply inevitable.

There were two princes in the township and everyone knew there could only be one king. I could sense what was coming and the time for the struggle to begin was growing short.

Popeye was a good-sized dog, seventy-five, maybe eighty pounds. Bum was up to fifty-nine pounds and after a very big meal, maybe sixty. Popeye was a German Shepherd. He was grayish-white in color with a long black muzzle.

The Shepherd was generally disliked by most people. He got into garbage cans, dug in flower beds, picked on smaller dogs, bit his next-door neighbor, and frightened most kids. It was not hard to understand why many people in Union Township disliked him. He simply had a nasty streak about him. However, I blamed the dog's behavior on his owner, and not on Popeye.

Hard as I tried, I never liked Henry Hostettler. My mother told me I should do all I could to be friends with him, but somehow it never worked out. Hostettler with his gang of hoods, along with Popeye, would roam the streets of the township and sometimes traveled into New Castle.

Rome Beltrone was sure that Hostettler had stolen his bicycle but could never prove it. The bike was sold to a kid from the east side of New Castle. However, the kid wouldn't tell anyone who sold him the bike, so the whole affair just faded away.

Johnny McCann saw Hostettler break two windows in his house the day before Halloween last year. But Hostettler had four friends that said Johnny was wrong. The affair ended in a four-to-one vote for Hostettler and again the entire incident was dropped.

Hostettler and his group seemed to enjoy punishing smaller kids and breaking up property. There were bad feelings building up and everyone knew how it was going to be resolved.

That day the entire gang traveled with me. Will, Johnny, Rome, and Charlie were there, and, of course, Bum. We would rather have gone after Hostettler's bunch of friends, but Bum and Popeye had other ideas. They insisted on being the main event.

Bum pulled at the leash as we moved down the street. He struggled to get free. Several times I told him "No." I held the leash tightly, but he was not interested in what I wanted. Bum had his own agenda.

"You guys must be nuts comin' over here! Bum is gonna knock that dog into the middle of next week and I ain't kiddin'," sneered Charlie.

"You think so, eh," scoffed one of Hostettler's friends. "You're the one that's nuts."

"I don't think so, I know so! He's gonna whip Popeye—you just wait till all this is over," snapped Charlie again.

"I think I'm gonna smack you right in the mouth," said Rome to one of Hostettler's pals. "You got it comin', you smart ass."

"Oh yeh?"

"Yeh," said Rome. "I been waitin' to do this a long time and this is as good a time as any."

"Well, go ahead and try it."

Will quietly moved closer to Rome's side. The expression on Will's face said everything. I knew he hated Hostettler and also knew Will loved a good fight. He moved closer still to show support for Rome. The two small groups were almost touching now and any little thing would set off an explosion.

"All right, you guys—knock it off!" I yelled. "We came to see these two dogs, remember? Now knock it off!"

Hostettler had stayed a short distance away with his dog. There would be no more waiting; the moment had come.

From across the street Popeye barked at us. That was all that was needed. Bum broke loose from me and Hostettler let go of Popeye. They met in the middle of the street like two raging African lions.

They rose up on their hind legs using their front paws like boxers. The snarling and growling was almost terrifying. White fangs flashed as each dog slammed into the other. Popeye, since he was heavier, tried to throw himself into Bum. Bum had gained some weight since their last contest, as well as gaining experience. Bum pushed back and circled to his right. Popeye was heavier, but it doesn't matter how much dog's in the fight—it only matters how much fight's in the dog.

Bum continued to circle to his right. Popeye continued to bore in and Bum kept circling and looking for that one opening. Popeye was courageous and fought on. The Shepherd was a noble foe, but this day he was going down.

Bum saw the opening. He drove into Popeye's ribs and pushed him sideways. Popeye struggled to keep his balance; he did not want to fall. But Bum knew the moment had come. He drove harder and harder, pushing the

Shepherd sideways. No longer could Popeye hold. Bum continued to drive hard and the big Shepherd went over onto the street.

Bum quickly went for the throat and he didn't let go. He would not let the Shepherd to his feet. There would be no second chances for Popeye. Bum had fought too hard to give any second chances for his larger foe.

For a moment I let him attack the bigger dog. I would stop it very soon, but I did not want there to be any doubt about who was the victor.

I approached the dogs, leaning over to take Bum's collar. But before I could get hold of the brown leather collar, Hostettler leaped toward the dogs and began kicking Bum.

"You dirty bastard," I thought to myself, "you dirty bastard!"

I've learned if you are absolutely certain you cannot avoid a fight, make certain you get in that first punch. It's very difficult for your opponent to fight with one eye closed. I swung my fist as hard as I could and got Hostettler's right eye. "Splat," was the sound and I just kept swinging.

Something snapped in me and I just kept punching him. I must've hit him thirty, forty, fifty times on his face and head. He went down hard on the brick street, but I did not stop swinging.

In the background I could hear Will and Charlie Rudolph. "Keep out of it, you guys. It's gonna be a fair fight just between these two. Keep out of it—you heard us!"

I jumped on Hostettler. He never hit me once. He covered his head with both arms. All he tried to do was protect his head and face.

There was blood on my shirt and hands but I kept punching away. Since his head was completely covered, I started on his body. I drove my fist deep into his ribs and I could hear him moan with each punch. I pounded away.

Then there was a terrible pain on my right ankle and lower leg and I let go of Hostettler. "Yeeoww," I screamed.

I could hear a dog snarling at me. Perhaps both dogs were attacking me. The pain was terrible and I grabbed my leg with both hands.

As I let go of him, Hostettler jumped to his feet. He raced down the street as fast as his feet would carry him. His friends and Popeye followed him and they all disappeared around the corner.

My leg was broken—I was sure of it. Up to that point and since that time I have never felt such pain. If a large truck had driven over my leg it could not have hurt me more. It was broken and I could not get up.

Looking up, I saw Bum was about four or five feet in front of me. Next to him were Will, Johnny, Rome, and Charlie Rudolph. Hostettler and his group had totally disappeared.

"What happened?" I moaned, still holding my leg.

"Bum bit you in the leg," said Johnny.

"Bum, you dirty rotten black and tan varmint, I hate you!"

I grabbed in the street for a nearby stone and I threw it at him as hard as I could, but missed. Neither my yelling at him nor my throwing the stone impressed him. He never moved, despite my yelling, and did not get within arm's reach of me. Bum was no dummy.

"He didn't mean to bite you," said Rome. "He obviously was trying to bite Hostettler. He just got the wrong leg and you can't be angry with him for that!"

"I don't care what he was trying to do – he broke my leg."

"He didn't break your leg," said Rome. "A dog bite can't break your leg. Maybe a lion or tiger bite—not a dog bite!"

"I can't walk. I can't even get up!"

"You'll be able to walk," said Rome. "It'll just hurt a day or two."

"That's easy for you guys to say—it's my leg that's busted."

"Jim, it was a great fight," said Charlie. "I knew Bum would win, but I gotta git goin'. It's almost supper time."

"Me too," said Johnny.

"Bum's the champ!" said Rome. "There's no doubt about that now. But if I'm late for supper, my mom will not understand."

"I'll walk home with you," said Will. "I'll help ya—you're gonna need some help."

"I can't walk on this. I'm sure it's broken, it hurts somethin' awful."

"It's not broken. Come on, let me help you up. Grab my hand, hold tight and don't slip."

The pain was terrible as I got to my feet. I could feel a little blood run down my ankle. Yet I knew that Will was right. I'd limp for a couple of days, but it wasn't broken.

This contest pushed Bum's reputation to its zenith. The Popeye bout, as it was later known, seemed to grow and grow each time it was told.

There were no coyotes or wolves in Union Township. Of course there were none; Bum had driven them out. The stories grew and grew and with each story Bum's reputation grew. People began to say they felt safer because Bum lived in the boundaries of our township.

Someone started a story that the New Castle Police Department wanted to buy Bum to patrol their streets and make the city safer. Of course, I couldn't sell Bum. His popularity was too great and public opinion would never let me do it. His name was as well-known as Babe Ruth's, Jack Dempsey's or Jim Thorpe's.

Bum was more popular than anything that came out of Hollywood. Lassie and Rin Tin Tin were second-raters compared to him now.

Stories about him continued to grow. He could swim faster than Johnny Weissmuller and could run faster than the great horse Man O' War. Tales about him simply would not stop. Someone wanted Bum to run for public office, but I never thought he'd like it very much.

The biggest story had Bum swimming in a race across Lake Erie. He respectfully declined. People even gave him credit for that. Folks said he was just being humble and didn't want to make other swimmers look bad.

There was no end to his popularity. The stories continued and I even started a few of them myself.

Strangely enough, the Popeye bout was Bum's last canine contest. He never had another fight. There was no need; anything after Popeye would've been a step down.

As Bum meandered down our streets, small dogs just scurried away; medium-sized dogs stood silently, letting him pass; heavy-weights knew if he had whipped Popeye they had no chance of handling him. He was now the undefeated champ of our township.

At the pinnacle of his career, Bum decided to retire. Bouts with Popeye no longer had any appeal. It was the close of a chapter in his life. He was changing–he had discovered girls.

From time to time, handsome black and tan Airedale puppies popped up in the area. In barber shops, grocery stores, and gas stations conversations began about these attractive youngsters. Who did they belong to and from where were they coming? Almost everyone seemed to talk about them. People talked about these pups more than the 1927 Yankees. I smiled, listened, yet never said a word. I was the cat that had swallowed the canary, but I had no doubt what their family background was.

• • •

Years later Hostettler apologized for the entire incident. He was sorry and acknowledged who had been the better dog that day. I accepted his apology, but always wished Bum had been there too. I know he would've liked to have heard it.

Chapter XI

There is something unreal about that first day of school. Every student talks at once—or more accurately, everyone yells at once. No one listens to anyone else. Everyone speaks quickly, as if time was limited and everything has to be told before time runs out. Everything done in the three summer months has to be told—nothing can be ignored or forgotten.

Every new piece of clothing purchased during the summer has to be described in great detail. Every baseball game, every tennis match, every swimming event, every contest has to be recalled. If you were on the winning team, the event is slowly told in much detail. If you were on the losing side, the outcome of the match simply is not mentioned.

Will and I would not participate in this madness. We arrived at school together but quickly separated. I went to my new locker and Will went to the office for the lunch schedule.

My locker was clean and smelled fresh. All summer the custodian had swept and cleaned lockers and hallways. It was probably the only day all school year my locker would be this hygienic, so I placed my books in it neatly and enjoyed it as long as possible, even if it would only be for a day or two.

Several people smiled and spoke to me as they passed my locker. Two guys from Hostettler's little group passed my locker and both of them acknowledged me. They didn't exactly speak, but they nodded their heads and I nodded back. It had been nearly six months since the Popeye bout and most of the hostility between the two groups had passed. Neither group taunted the other any more, but everyone remembered who had been the victor.

Satisfied my locker was well stocked and everything was neatly in its place, I locked it. The lunch period was still twenty minutes away and I needed to kill some time.

Then I remembered the new gymnasium. Construction had begun in the spring months and was now nearly finished. I hurried down the long hallway to find it.

A paper sign hung in the huge doorway. It read: "Keep Out. Wet Floor." The shiny varnish on the floor was not thoroughly dry. The floor had a bright luster and the entire gym smelled new and fresh. On the other side of the gym was a huge stage with rose velvet curtains. On each side were twenty-five rows of seats that nearly reached the ceiling. It was beautiful with the rose velvet curtains—much more attractive than the old gym.

My interest in the new gymnasium began to wane. I wanted to walk up the rows of bleachers to the top row, but the sign in the doorway prohibited that. There was nothing much more to see and so I moved on.

The hallways were less crowded now; most of the kids had found somewhere to go. I spoke to a few more kids and continued to walk with no real destination in mind. Halfway to my locker I saw her.

As I approached she stood motionless and watched me from the other side of the hall. When I was only a few feet away a wonderful smile came to her face. Her brown eyes flashed at me.

"Hello," she said.

"Hi," I answered, with a small smile on my own face. "Thank you for filling in the hole in your yard. I never got a chance to thank you earlier. It was my dog who made that mess. Cleaning it up was a nice thing you did. Thank you."

"You're welcome."

"I sure hope it didn't get you into any trouble. I was afraid your father would be very upset."

"There was no trouble. After I leveled the dirt with the rake, I sprinkled some grass seed on it. You can't notice anything was ever there now."

"Thanks again."

"You're welcome again."

"Where are you going now?" I asked.

"To the cafeteria. Lunch should start in about five minutes and I am very hungry."

"Good. I'll walk with you; I'm going to the same place."

I took her hand. It seemed like the natural thing to do and I couldn't resist her anyway. I had to be careful. If the principal or any teacher saw us it would make serious trouble. We walked slowly next to the wall, letting everyone else walk around us. We continued to be careful. If we saw any teacher approach, I would instantly drop her hand. We turned the hallway toward the cafeteria and continued our slow pace.

In the distance down the hallway I saw some very familiar faces and they saw us. Charlie, Johnny, and Rome were almost directly in front of us. They dropped their eyes just enough to notice our hands together. I had no doubt they saw.

Their mouths dropped open. Their eyes were as big as saucers and they looked as if they had been struck by lightening. I was very calm.

As we passed each other, I spoke. "Hi guys, how are things goin'?"

They never said a word, but I thought I saw Rome wave his hand to me, but I wasn't even certain of that.

"What's the matter with those three?" asked Sally. "They acted so dopey. I've never seen them like that before."

"Why, nothing's the matter with them," I said, looking straight ahead and trying to look natural while lying through my teeth at the same time. I wanted to roar out loud but kept calm and very suave.

"They didn't even speak to us," she said. "That's not like them. They're usually very nice. They're certainly acting a little strange today."

"I think Rome waved to us."

"I didn't notice any wave. I didn't notice anything from the three of them. Maybe they are just excited about the first day of school."

When we reached the door of the cafeteria the entrance was very crowded. We stopped and waited. Sally turned and looked back at the three of them.

"What are they doing?" I asked.

"They're just staring at us with their mouths hanging open and that dopey look on their faces. I don't know what it is, but they have something on their minds."

"I'll explain it to you later, Sally. I'll explain it later—maybe after school."

"This certainly is an unusual first day of school," she said with a confused look on her face.

"It certainly is, sweetheart," I said, with a smile coming over my lips. "It certainly is."

Chapter XII

Rome Beltrone had a keen interest in several things: pretty girls; nice clothes; trout fishing; and tobacco, pretty much in that order. Of course he liked other things also, but they came far behind these four.

Rome took it hard when he saw Sally and me together. Obviously he had an interest in her for a long time. For a few weeks he had a hard time even speaking to me, but being a good friend, he let things get back to the old way.

The gang was picking up Bum and me and heading to a new spot. We had changed our hideout since our problems with the Italian cigars. They would be here at one o'clock and Rome was bringing new tobacco. There would be no more little Italian cigars. This time, Rome was bringing tobacco and cigarette paper. I had never rolled a cigarette before, but Rome would show us how it was done.

It was twelve-thirty when Bum and I sat down on the steps. I knew the time would pass slowly, but we had nothing else to do so we waited.

Bum went to the hedge at the front of the walk and calmly lifted his leg. Then he stood there erect, tail straight up, and looked up and down the street, seeming to know they were coming. He showed that same aloofness that I had noticed since the first day.

Will's father felt strongly that Bum was out of some registered pedigree show stock. His beautiful head, flat backline and general conformation were simply too good for this not to be true. He even possessed the attitude that he was special, the very thing that a handler wanted in the show ring.

There was a family in New Castle and three others in Pittsburgh that had Airedale kennels. Perhaps he had come from one of these four. But more than likely he had come from the large kennel in LaRue, Ohio.

My Uncle Henry felt strongly that he had come from breeding stock used in the Great War. It was no secret that the British and U.S. governments had used them as war dogs. The Germans had also used a few of them in the conflict.

Of course, we would never know—his lineage would be a mystery to us. But the biggest mystery was why no one had ever inquired about him. There were no lost and found articles and messages anywhere. No one had ever asked my father anything about him. I had long ago decided that if anyone tried to take him, we would simply run away together.

But the days of worrying about losing him had passed. We were both happy and secure where we were. He was mine, yet in a way he belonged to the five of us. His past had very little interest for us anymore. We lived for the moment.

From up the street I could hear their voices and knew they were coming. Bum heard them also, looked in their direction and wagged his tail.

"Are we goin' to the hideout?" I asked. "Which way are we headed–or has anyone decided that yet?"

"We're not gonna use that old hideout for awhile," said Rome. "We're going' to a new spot today."

"There's nothing wrong with that old hideout," said Charlie. "It was those cigars that jinxed us."

"Those cigars were okay," said Rome, "you guys just weren't used to them. That's why we're tryin' something different today."

"How many years you gotta smoke those little devils before you're used to them?" asked Will, with a tiny sneer on his lips.

"All right, you guys, let's forget about those cigars. Where are we goin' anyway?"

"To Henderson's farm," said Rome, "the very opposite side of the farm where the old hideout was."

"Why?" asked Johnny. "There's nothing there but a field."

"You'll find out when we get there," snipped Rome.

A short while later we arrived. Bum left the woods, went into the field and surveyed it thoroughly.

"I told ya there's nothin' here but a field," said Johnny.

"Oh yes, there is," said Rome. "Follow me and I'll show you the place."

Just inside the field was an unusual rock formation. The rocks could not be seen from anywhere outside and no one could even see that we were in the field. We each picked out our seats on the stones. The stones obviously had been put here many years ago. They had been here a long time, perhaps even from the Revolutionary War days.

"Show me how to roll this cigarette, Rome," said Will. "I never did this before. I always smoked the ones already made."

Will had spilled a considerable amount of tobacco on the stones trying to make just one cigarette.

"Careful with that stuff, Will," said Rome, "I didn't bring that much! You're throwin' it around like we got a bushel basket full." Each of us picked up some of the shredded tobacco Will had dropped. We did our best with the little cigarettes. They didn't look very pretty, but they smoked pretty good—a lot milder than those Italian cigars.

Because we had left so much air in the tobacco, the little white paper burned quickly and each cigarette didn't last very long. And so we lit a second and a third. Each one tasted better than the last, and so we smoked another. The soft blue smoke rose seven or eight feet in the air and the wind took it away.

"Rome, this is pretty good stuff," said Charlie. "They don't look so good, but I like 'em. I like 'em a lot."

"So do I," I agreed. "I gotta learn to get better at rollin' 'em, but the flavor's pretty good."

"Thanks," said Rome, with a little smile on his face.

Bum began to bark. He continued to bark, again and again.

"Jim, what's that dog barkin' at?" asked Johnny.

"I got no idea."

"Look!" shouted Will. "That's what he's barkin' at." He pointed to the field behind us.

We turned to see and it was our worst nightmare. Somehow we had managed to set the field on fire! We could smell it now. The flames were a foot high, and they ravaged the dead, dry weeds.

"Come on, you guys," I shouted, "we gotta get this fire put out."

We tried to stomp it and for a short while we succeeded, but slowly the flames got too big. They burned the soles of our tennis shoes—even our legs. The flames continued to grow. Now they were too high and too hot. We fought on, but we were losing—we were losing badly.

"Jim, we gotta get out of here!" yelled Will.

"If we do, the whole field will go up."

"It doesn't matter—it's gonna go anyway," yelled Will. "We can't stop it! It's too big! We've lost."

"We gotta try!"

"He's right, Jim," yelled Johnny. "The whole field is gonna go. We gotta go and we gotta go right now!"

"Jim, they're right!" yelled Charlie. "It's too hot! I don't know how it started, but it's over. It's over! Let's get outa here!"

We ran through the woods as fast as we could. Bum led the way. Our faces were whipped by some of the tree branches and multi-flora rose bushes, but we kept going. I looked back one last time. The smoke was high now and very black. It swirled as it rose and drifted as far as I could see. The field would burn on and on—it was totally gone. I had no idea where the end of the field was, but wherever it was, it was a long way off. There was no doubt it would burn to the end.

•   •   •

The pendulum swung slowly. The old clock clicked steadily as it hung on the wall of the judge's chambers. The walnut desk before us had all the characteristics of a tiny fortress. On top of it were books, papers, pencils and a variety of things. It must've been the largest desk in the world.

As fast as we had run from the field, it had not been fast enough. We had almost made it—almost. A woman had seen us running from the woods and recognized Charlie. He was the only one she recognized and he was enough.

The judge entered through the courtroom door and he still wore his black robe. Quietly and yet respectfully, we all stood. He looked at each one of us. He stood for nearly a minute before he spoke.

"Sit down, boys."

He sat behind the walnut desk and held a single sheet of paper. His face was expressionless and he gave not the slightest hint of what he felt. Very calmly, he read our names in alphabetical order.

"Romeo Beltrone, William Franklin, John McCann, Charles Rudolph, and James Ryhal, are you all present?" he asked.

"Yes, sir," we answered in unison.

"Now, young men, this is very serious business. Burning down a field, destruction of property, and trespassing are involved. Does anyone have anything to say? I'm willing to listen."

"Your honor," said Will softly, "the burning of that field was a complete accident. No one meant to do that. Doesn't that count for something?"

"You boys burned part of a standing wheat field before the fire department could get there and extinguish it. That means someone lost part of a cash crop. It also means that some farmer lost a considerable amount of money."

"Your honor," said Charlie, "we weren't trespassing. You see, Mr. Henderson had given us permission many times to be on his property. We have sort of a little hideout in his woods."

"Young man, you are mistaken. You were trespassing! You had passed over John Henderson's farm onto the McKissick farm. You burned Thomas McKissick's field and part of his wheat field. The Henderson property ended at the woods."

There it was and Will and Charlie had nothing more to say. Johnny, Rome and I had said nothing during the entire conversation. Now all five of us fell silent. I looked at the other four. Their heads were down and they stared at the floor.

The door to the side of the office opened partially and some officer of the court, in some sort of police uniform, spoke to the judge. "Your Honor, there's a dog out here. If we go to the juvenile detention center, should I take him? I don't know what to do with this animal."

I couldn't believe my ears! He was asking if he should take Bum to jail with us! The thought of Bum looking out through the bars was simply unbelievable. The judge and the uniformed officer continued to speak but I no longer listened. If they were going to send an innocent dog to jail, there was no telling how long they might keep us there. Everything I imagined became worse.

"We'll discuss that later, Bailiff," said the judge. "We're discussing some other things right now. Just keep the animal here for now. I'll answer your question a little later."

"Yes sir," said the bailiff as he closed the heavy door.

The judge stayed seated behind his desk. He glanced at several pages of court papers and then spoke slowly.

"Have any of you young fellows ever been in the Boy Scouts?"

The five of us looked at each other with blank stares. Then after a short time, we looked again at the judge and slowly shook our heads "no."

"The Boy Scouts are really a great organization. There are a whole group of great activities they do. Mostly they teach leadership and citizenship." He kept talking.

What the hell is he talking about, I wondered. *Has this judge lost his mind? Has he forgotten why we're here? Has he forgotten this is his office?* I worried about my dog and the five of us going to jail and he's talking about the Boy Scouts! He kept talking about badges, medals, ribbons and Eagle Scouts. I just didn't get it. What was he driving at?

"I always wanted to be a Boy Scout," said Will, with a ridiculous look on his face. "They really do some great things. I always wanted to join." Will kept talking.

What's the matter with Will? He's started talking like some goofball! The judge has got him talking that way now.

"I always liked their uniforms," said Rome. "Those brown uniforms with brass medals and gold braid really look sharp. I know I'd look good in one. Long pants in the winter and short pants in the summer. Isn't that right, Judge?"

"I think so," said the judge.

Oh no! I couldn't believe my ears! *He's got Rome talking like a goofball now. We always knew Rome liked nice clothes, but now he's lost his mind. Boy Scout uniforms? Short pants?*

Will, Rome and the judge kept talking. It was as if Charlie, Johnny and I weren't even in the room. They had their little three-way thing goin' and that was all that mattered. The whole scene was out of a three-ring circus.

"Will they let a colored kid in the Scouts?" asked Johnny. "I don't think they'll let me in, Judge."

"Don't you worry about that, young man. I'll take care of that," answered the judge.

I glanced at Johnny trying to get some answers. He looked back at me with a blank expression on his face. Then a tiny smile came to his lips and he winked at me.

What's with the tiny smile? And what does that wink mean? I must be the dumbest kid in the whole world–I still didn't get it.

And then the light went on. Was the judge offering us the choice between juvenile court and the Boy Scouts?

That was it! He didn't want us going to juvenile court any more than we did. No jail—for us or Bum.

Will, Rome, and the judge kept talking. The other three of us just listened and smiled at each other. There was no need for us to add anything. Will and Rome had things under control.

I looked at Charlie and he was smiling now. I must've really been a dope, but Charlie got the idea last—even after me! It didn't matter. We felt as if giant weights had been taken from our backs and we might rise to the ceiling like hot-air balloons.

"Now you can't join the Scouts for only a few weeks, don't misunderstand me," snapped the judge. "They want Scouts for a long time. They want Scouts for two or three years, usually even more."

We all nodded to the judge. We got the picture. Anything to keep us out of juvenile court. We were signing up for the long haul.

And that's how we all ended up in the Boy Scouts—even Bum. He became the mascot for Troop 37.

Chapter XIII

Somewhere hidden in the deep recesses of most mothers' hearts is the dream that their sons will be world-renowned musicians. Many mothers wish their sons would be classical pianists. Others urge their sons to play a lovely brass instrument, like a French horn, a trombone, or even a trumpet. Others urge their sons to be vocalists. Some hope that one day their sons will be composers or directors. My mother insisted I play the violin.

When she first approached me about this I did not feel negative. I did not feel positive. I did not feel anything. From the tips of my toes upwards, I was numb. I had been to the family dentist several times and had several teeth filled. My body reacted as though my mother had used a gigantic syringe and injected me with novocaine.

My mother continued to talk about this wonderful stringed instrument. It would teach me discipline, sophistication, and an appreciation for all the arts. My sisters both played the piano and they were very glad they did. However, she felt something else was better for me. She chose the violin with the possibility of duets with the piano.

My mother was usually not a talkative person, but today she was totally out of character. She talked a long time, perhaps twenty minutes. Every several minutes she would stop and look at me. It appeared as if she were soliciting some response from me because her pauses were regular. Each time I was silent. Of course she continued to look at my mouth, which was locked in the half-open position from the novocaine.

"Is there anything wrong, Jimmy?" she asked. "You haven't said a single word. Isn't there something you want to ask me?"

I shook my head back and forth for my answer. I seemed to be unable to say anything, but she understood what I meant. She continued her monologue with occasional breaks for my response. I said nothing and she kept talking. From this point on I never heard anything more she said. I heard sounds, but not words with any understanding.

It was not all clear in my mind exactly what a violin was. I had some vague images of stringed instruments in my mind. Was it like a guitar, a banjo or a harp? My worst fear was that it was that huge thing that was taller than I was. If it was that thing, how would I get it in and out of the house?

Although I could not picture the instrument, there was little doubt in my mind what my friends would think. Rome would probably show no emotion since he already played the piano. He might be laughing on the inside but simply not show it, since he knew I would make some crack about the piano. Johnny would probably have some small smirk when he heard. He played the trumpet and felt any other instrument was a big step downward.

Will and Charlie would be something else! They would not even try to hide their laughter and contempt. Their laughter would resemble the roar at a football game when the home team scored. Somehow I'd have to live with it.

• • •

Dr. Muhlenberg must've been eight feet tall. However, my mother assured me that he was only six feet, seven inches. He had come to America about twelve years before the armistice was signed ending the Great War. He had arrived around 1906 and spoke with a very strong German accent, which he kept for his lifetime.

Why they called him Dr. Muhlenberg, I never knew. He certainly wasn't a medical doctor. The title had something to do with music, but I could never figure out what it was. I always called him Dr. Muhlenberg, because my mother told me it was the respectful thing to do.

Many people were not so kind to Dr. Muhlenberg. Some folks called him "Kraut" Muhlenberg or "the Rotten Hun." Someone had abused his little Dachshund in 1918 before the war ended and the little dog died.

My mother was very firm against me ever saying or doing anything disrespectful toward him or anyone in his family. She reminded me that her own grandparents had come to America less than a century before from Germany. I never heard anyone use nasty terms for my violin teacher, but probably would have found it difficult to hide my anger if they had.

Strangely, I began to like the violin. The first two or three lessons found me indifferent, but as I slowly mastered it, I liked it more and more. I no longer created excuses not to practice the instrument, but actually looked forward to it. I usually practiced immediately after I got home from school.

The only time Bum was permitted upstairs in our home was when I practiced. I never knew why my parents permitted this, and I did not ask from fear that they might change this new-found privilege. Bum would sit erect on his rump and watch me intently. Only the two of us were in the living room at these times. He would sit near Hazel's grand piano and act as if I created some sort of magic. Perhaps my mother permitted the dog in the living room hoping it would help me practice regularly. Perhaps she was right.

Occasionally Bum would raise his muzzle slightly toward the ceiling and make an unusual sound. He opened his mouth just a little and went *roa-rooooo*. I never understood whether it was a negative complaint or a sign of approval. Perhaps he was singing. Perhaps he didn't know why he did it at all. But whatever reason he did it, I never discouraged him. From time to time he tilted his head from one side to the other. I never understood what that meant either. But he never missed a practice and he never left early.

My practices certainly helped my performance. Dr. Muhlenberg often praised me. He would say, "Keep up ze goot verk, James." And so I continued to practice religiously and kept up "ze goot verk."

After about six months I began to arrive early for my lessons. My lessons did not begin any earlier, but I came early to listen to the young man whose lesson was before mine. He played beautifully. My own skills were improving and I was becoming very good, but I never quite reached the level of Anthony.

The two of us began our training on the violin at the same time, but he played better and was a notch ahead of me from our beginnings. My technique and determination to work hard had closed the gap in our playing. Yet I was never able to reach the level of his playing.

Anthony Cambaro played as if the violin was part of him, an extension of his body. He attained a fluidity in his movement that I never quite reached. I played well, advanced in my work, but I was always second to him. There were many students learning under Dr. Muhlenberg—perhaps eighteen or twenty. I was happy that I learned more and played better than all of them—except Anthony.

Anthony and I appreciated each other's playing, but most of all, we became friends. He and I were very much unalike. Anthony had never shot a BB gun. He had never squeezed the trigger of a .22 rifle. He had never fired a shotgun. He had never used a bow and arrow. He rarely went swimming and had gone fishing only once in his life. But I never talked down to him about any of these things and it surely cemented our friendship.

Almost a year after our first lessons, Anthony invited me to his home for dinner. Over the years I was invited and accepted the invitation many times. He had told me what a great cook his mother was. Already I loved Italian food and was excited about going to his home. At the same time, I was a little apprehensive about that first visit. How should I dress? How should I act? Should I talk much or leave that all to Anthony?

My knuckles knocked on his front door. I knocked again. Anthony answered the door and took me into the living room. After several minutes his mother entered the room and smiled, and I said, "Hello." I arose from the sofa as I spoke to her.

His mother was very nice. She was small, petite, even tiny—shorter than Anthony or me. She had very dark hair and if she weighed over a hundred pounds, I would've been very surprised.

She led us into the dining room to a large walnut dining table. Anthony sat at one end of the long table and I sat at the other end. His father was traveling, and since Anthony had no brothers or sisters, only the two of us ate. Because there were only two of us, the large table seemed even larger. His mother served us, but did not eat.

The sauce on the spaghetti was delicious. The meatballs were sweet and were soon gone. The hot bread melted the butter and both melted in my mouth. It was wonderful and before I realized, my plate was empty.

"James, your plate is empty!"

"No, no, thank you. I couldn't hold—"

Before I could finish my sentence, there was more spaghetti, sauce, and meatballs on my plate. Several moments later, she brought a second plate entirely filled with bread, placed it next to my glass of water, and left the room.

At our meals at home the food was almost always passed around the table. Then it was every man for himself. At our table, I quickly drove my fork into the best piece of meat to get it before the plate even reached my sisters. In our home, when your plate was empty you chose what more you wanted.

In Anthony's home the meals were served in the continental style. It was European—from the old country. Women served the guest—particularly men. Despite our young age, we were the princes of the household.

I glanced at Anthony. He frowned at me and slowly shook his head from side to side. I understood him quickly. If I didn't want any more food, I shouldn't completely empty my plate. If I did, his mother thought I wanted more food and continued her serving. At our home we were taught to clean up our plates. In Anthony's home cleaning up all your food was not exactly the best idea unless you desired more and more.

Now I understood why his mother was so shapely and petite; she never ate anything. All her time was spent serving. She rarely ate her own cooking. Her time was spent going from the dining room to the kitchen and then back again.

Anthony had learned this game a long time ago. My stomach felt close to bursting, but at least I'd learned the game. I could hold no more. Yet I ate one more piece of warm bread and butter. His mother came back from the kitchen.

"James, don't you like the dinner?"

"It's wonderful. I like it very much!"

"Good. Eat from your plate and I'll bring you more bread and spaghetti."

"No, thank you. I can't. I just can't hold any more."

"I have more bread for you."

"Thank you. No! I can eat no more."

At last she understood. She smiled and left the dining room. In less than a minute she returned with two plates. She served me first and then Anthony. On each plate was the largest piece of German chocolate cake I had ever seen. I could eat no more, yet somehow I managed to make that cake disappear.

Over the years I had dinner many times at the Cambaros'. Each time it seemed better. His mother was wonderful to us, each time never eating a meal herself.

Anthony came many times to our house on Moore Avenue. My bedroom fascinated him. The pictures of fish, models of biplanes and battleships, ball gloves, and fishing poles—he never grew bored. He liked my BB gun and .22 rifle, but most of all, he liked Bum.

Anthony and Bum were truly strange bedfellows. In his rough-and-tumble way, Bum was even more unlike Anthony than I was. But since he had no dog of his own, Anthony adored Bum. He talked to him, petted him, played ball with him and did not wish to give him up. From time to time we'd play with a different toy, but the interest in the toy would quickly wane. Anthony would find some reason to desert the plane or the model ship and find his way back to Bum.

Anthony was the only person besides myself from whom Bum would take commands. No one in the gang could get him to be obedient. Anthony had gotten Bum to sit, stay, lie down, come, and fetch a tennis ball. They were real friends.

After high school Anthony and I never saw each other again. We parted good friends, but our lives took completely different paths and it was somewhat sad. I gave up the violin, but he did not. Anthony became a wonderful violinist and later a conductor.

It was not difficult to follow his career in music. I read of him often in our local newspaper and had friends whose children took lessons from him. It's amazing that we never crossed paths again. It seemed natural that we would've bumped into each other somewhere, in a restaurant, a clothing store, or a gas station, but we never did.

Later I left town and moved to Erie. But I never forgot what a neat guy he was and how much I had learned from him. And anyone who liked Bum that much had to be a special person.

Chapter XIV

The thermometer had read ninety-seven degrees Fahrenheit yesterday in our backyard. In our kitchen it was one hundred twenty degrees Fahrenheit where my mother canned fruits and vegetables for the Lutheran Children's Home in Zelienople. She continuously wiped away perspiration from her forehead, but this did not slow her or distract her from her work. I think she spent half her life in our kitchen.

The following day was ninety degrees. It was the hottest June on record and everyone was fearful of what the heat would be in late July and August. Despite the temperature she spent most of her daylight hours in the kitchen again. My mother could cook everything and cook it well. My family loved her meals and always told her so.

Her roast beef, mashed potatoes, and gravy was a big favorite. There was never any of it left. I always got more than my share of the rich, dark brown gravy. Her homemade bread was wonderful; with butter, peanut butter, apple butter, strawberry jam or by itself.

The fish from the Neshannock were never wasted. We liked it broiled, baked or fried. Sometimes I had pan-fried trout for breakfast with home-fried potatoes and biscuits. Occasionally the jam fell from my biscuits onto the fish and made its flavor even better.

My mother's maiden name was Dorothea Miller. Her grandparents had made the ocean voyage from Germany. She prepared traditional German foods, but all of us, including my mother, liked Italian food just as much. Once a month we usually had lasagna or spaghetti with meatballs. The meatballs were sweet and the sauce was rich.

Today was my favorite—stuffed turkey. I liked all my mother's dishes, but roast stuffed fowl was the best. Occasionally we had pheasant or wild duck. The fragrance permeated the entire house. With the turkey there were little red potatoes, green vegetables, fruit, hot bread, and of course, stuffing. Most of the day it roasted slowly and you could smell its goodness even outside the house. We did not have turkey simply on Thanksgiving Day.

The aroma from the kitchen was like a magnet that pulled me into the room. Any little tidbit to find I quickly got. My mother knew my tricks and as she took plates of food from the kitchen to the dining room, I followed her.

"James, I don't want you following me in here," she said emphatically. "I want you out of the kitchen and out of the dining room and I want it right now. It would be easier on both of us if you would even get out of the house for a little while."

There was no room for debate—she was right. I could smell the sweet fragrance from the outside, but not as easily as when I was in the kitchen.

Bum stood at the bottom of the back steps. He stayed near the kitchen also. He could smell the roasting bird even better than I could. He was no dummy and knew there would be a few tasty morsels in his bowl tonight on top of his regular food.

The two of us sat quietly together like two hungry wolves waiting our turn. We could hear Hazel and Allison in the kitchen as they carried the food to the dining room.

Bum rolled his dark eyes at me. He knew that additional voices meant the time was near and he had been through this waiting ritual before. I tied him to the henhouse.

My father returned thanks and I was grateful for short prayers. I had waited all afternoon for this regal meal. I would've been just as happy to eat the cherry pie first, but I knew that would not be permitted by either parent.

The food was passed around the table. I waited patiently and took each portion. Of course I took larger portions of that which I felt would be eaten faster. Bread and green beans could wait. Slabs of turkey breast, red potatoes covered with rich gravy, and stuffing I ate first.

Some families talk a great deal at this type of large meal. For those families it was more of a social and conversational affair. Our family meals were not that way. The long preparation time my mother had given made us not want to wait an extra second. When we were served, we wasted little time talking. Of course, I always wanted to eat my share of certain foods before my sisters got to them. All of our eating was attributed to my mother. We knew she was the finest cook in the world and conversation came to an end when we sat down.

"Jim, where is Bum?" asked my father.

"I tied him right before I came in."

"Where did you tie him?"

"Where I always do. I tied him to the front of the henhouse. He's there; do you want me to go back and look?"

"No, I'll take your word for it. I want you to keep tying him there. I want him tied for the next two weeks—maybe three. Do you understand me?"

"Yes, sir. He'll be tied. I'll keep him right there at the henhouse. He'll be tied."

My father picked at his lower teeth with a tiny wooden toothpick. He held the toothpick in his hand and spoke again. "There is some word going around that someone is throwing out poisoned meat. It may be just a rumor or it may not. The important thing is to keep Bum tied whether the rumor is true or not."

"Why would anyone throw out meat with poison in it?" asked Allison. "I just don't understand that. It makes no sense at all."

"Someone has a female dog in season," said my father. "It may not be true about the poison. I'm not saying it is true. But if you keep Bum tied for awhile, he'll be safe."

"That's the most terrible thing I ever heard!" said Hazel. "Why don't they keep their dog in the cellar or tied in the garage for a time? They should be more responsible! To run the risk of painfully killing some innocent dog is terrible—it's the worst thing I ever heard!"

"It is terrible," said my mother. "If it's true, you should be upset, Hazel. But it may not be true—we don't know, we just don't know."

"The important thing is to keep Bum tied," said Father. "If everyone does that, things will be all right. Jim, you be certain to do the right thing."

"I still think it's hateful," said Hazel. "The idea of someone arbitrarily killing some innocent animal is awful! It's just dreadful! Can't we contact the sheriff or someone? There's got to be a law against doing such an awful thing!"

"Yes, Hazel, you can contact the sheriff if you have any evidence," said Father. "You would have to see someone do it. Obviously, if someone was doing it, they'd be certain to watch and be sure no one saw them doing it. And besides, we still aren't certain if the story is even true or not. We have to be certain it is true before we set out to accuse someone. The most important thing we can do is be certain that Bum is tied and on our property."

"Your father is right," said Mother. "Be certain our dog is tied and safe. Now let's talk about something more pleasant, rather than worrying about something that may not even be true."

It was the first time I'd ever heard someone in my family ever refer to Bum as "our dog." It felt wonderful knowing that everyone in the family cared about him. Of course the gang and I felt that way, and it was good to see others felt that same way about him also.

I poured the turkey gravy over Bum's food. Under the gravy were pieces of turkey, stuffing, a few green beans, and potatoes—all going on top of his dog food.

I stepped back several paces and watched him eat. He ate it slowly and ate it all. I was happy to know he was satisfied. For perhaps the first time, I fully understood how much I loved him.

Chapter XV

It seems to me that every person has a special place from their youth that they never forget. It is that place where friends met—the old hangout. Some kids remember a gymnasium or a baseball diamond. For some it's a swimming hole, a lake, or a municipal swimming pool. For others it's their favorite skating rink or dance hall. Our special place was the hill.

For eight months out of the year the hill was hardly noticed. It was home to sparrows, robins, and cardinals. The grass was perfect for rabbits. Many young rabbits were only as big as your fist, only a month old, but they survived. Now and then you could see a hen pheasant leave the hill followed by her brood of seven or eight chicks.

Whitetail deer would occasionally be seen on the hill. They didn't live there, for the grass was too short for hiding cover, but there were sweet grasses and acorns from the nearby oak trees on the edge of the hill. These things drew the deer.

With the first snowflakes in late November, our hill came alive with kids. It was perfect for sledding, the best hill in Union Township, and one of the best in all Lawrence County. Every kid in the township had used the hill at one time or another.

It was a few days after Christmas, that week between Christmas and New Year's, and of course school was out. The snow was packed and a little hard, just right for sledding. There were sleds of all kinds, sizes, and colors that day. There were toboggans and some kids actually brought huge pieces of cardboard to use. The weather was perfect, bright and cold. It couldn't have been more than a few degrees above zero that day, but we loved it.

At the bottom of the hill was a small stream, and it was frozen solid. When sled riding on most hills, you simply stopped at the bottom. This was not true on our hill. When your sled hit the frozen stream, you took off even faster, creating more excitement.

There were many exciting days I'd been to the hill, but this day was the most memorable. There were over a hundred kids at the hill that day. Every kid I knew in Union Township was there and a few I didn't recognize. A group of kids from New Castle came out to sled ride with us. They had friends and relatives in the township. There were too many kids on the hill and it had become dangerous.

Sally had come with a new toboggan, a brand new Christmas gift. She always looked good to us, but this day she looked even better. Her cheeks were red from the cold, matching her coat. Her blond hair flowing over the collar of her coat made it impossible not to notice her. She had brought two friends, and Rome and Charlie were glad. Will, Johnny, and Bum were there also. Even Hostettler and his friends were there; it had become a big show.

There was a certain procedure you should follow at the hill. Most kids knew the procedure. The first-time visitors didn't know the procedure, so didn't follow it.

After you finished your ride, you quickly moved to the edges of the hill. As you walked up the edges for your next ride you kept away from the middle. If you went to the center of the hill, you took your life in your hands.

As I walked up the far edge of the hill pulling my sled, I saw Sally going down. She was on her long toboggan with her two girlfriends and Bum. They held him tightly as his ears blew straight out in the wind. It was apparent from the look on his face that Bum did not appreciate the ride.

At the bottom of the hill the toboggan hit the frozen stream, gained speed and plowed into a huge snow drift. The girls held on, but Bum went flying into the snowbank, completely submerged. Fighting his way out of the drift, he stood erect, shaking the snow from his ears, and for several minutes shook vigorously. After this ride, no one could get him on a sled or toboggan again.

Now Bum became a nuisance. When Bum got hard-headed, no one could be a bigger nuisance. He darted into the middle of the hill. He either didn't realize or didn't care what a precarious place it was. I don't think he really cared. To him the middle of the hill was now a racetrack and every sledder was a target for him to catch.

"Somebody get that dog outa here," yelled one of Hostettler's friends as he raced down the hill.

Bum kept chasing anyone who passed him. Halfway down the hill, he started up again, looking for another target. The sleds were too fast and that seemed to drive him with more determination to grab a boot or shoe as it passed.

"Jimmy, get Bum out of here!" yelled Sally. "He's going to get hurt badly."

She was right, but there was no way for anyone to enter that line of sleds. The traffic actually got worse. At the top of the hill kids were not even waiting a few seconds for kids at the bottom to get out of the way. As soon as one group started down, others followed immediately.

Near the frozen stream at the bottom of the hill, two girls were crying. Someone had given them no chance to move and had plowed into them. Four boys were arguing, a punch was thrown, and the fight was on.

"Get that dog the hell out of here," someone yelled again. Too many sleds, too many kids, and one too many Airedales—things were out of control.

Bum dodged sleds and kept moving. Kids strained hard at the handles of their sleds to miss Bum and to miss each other. What happened next was inevitable, and it was a miracle it hadn't happened earlier.

In the middle of the hill a large red Flexible Flyer caught Bum from behind. He went into the air and actually landed on the back of a small girl guiding her sled. He rode about thirty feet on her back before falling off. Immediately he was struck again by a toboggan. Now he went rolling end over end on the hard snow. He fell over on his side and continued to slide all the way to the bottom.

Bum came to a stop in the middle of the small frozen stream. Next to him was the small girl on whose sled he'd been a passenger. The girl was dazed and looked at Bum. She had given him a ride and yet had little idea exactly what had happened.

The huge crowd began to break up; kids were getting frightened. They were afraid of hurting someone and of getting hurt themselves. In all directions, kids started for home, pulling their sleds behind.

Sally and her friends waved goodbye to us and then headed home in the opposite direction. Rome and Charlie wanted to walk with them, but we were in no condition to spend extra time walking with anyone. Our feet ached terribly from the cold; I never remember my feet ever being that cold again. We walked with a painful numbness to each step.

"I'll never be warm again," said Johnny. "I'll never be warm next summer, if I live to see next summer."

"Quit your moanin', John," said Will. "You're not that cold! You'll feel good tomorrow. Wait and see."

"No I won't! I know I won't."

We all limped along. The distance to home seemed twice as far. The snow crunched beneath our feet as we kept going. The cold was terrible, but we kept moving. Bum limped the most. He was very fortunate that his two back legs had not been broken. We would probably feel fine tomorrow, but Bum would probably need an extra day—maybe two. It had been a good day; it simply had not ended quite the way we had planned.

Chapter XVI

Each year I grew better playing basketball. After I broke my leg playing football the previous fall, my mother announced she would never sign the permission letter for the football team at Union High. I was very disappointed; however, I knew she would never change her mind about this. Consequently, I worked even harder playing basketball, concentrating on it almost exclusively.

Basketball, baseball, and tennis were now my favorite sports, in that order. In early September, I yearned for the contact of football. I missed the game. But I knew it was out of the question, and therefore used September and October for practice time for the basketball season that began in late November.

St. John's Lutheran had a good team in the New Castle Church League. Rome and I were the guards on the team and Sally's younger brother Butch jumped center for us. At six feet, four inches, he was the tallest player in our league. Last year we had had a good team, but with the addition of Butch we were favored to win the league championship. This had been an exciting year. With our team's speed and defense, along with Butch's rebounding, we were now 14 - 1. We had absolutely given away a game to a small church team earlier in the season. We should have been undefeated but deserved the loss. We had taken that team lightly and had learned our lesson.

Our coach was not going to let that happen again. We grew angry each time we talked about that game, and agreed not to mention that loss to each other again. It became the great motivator for us to win our one remaining game.

Epworth was a good team. They were also 14 - 1. We had beaten them earlier in the season but by only four points. It was our best game of the season—and probably their best game also. They were a good bunch of Methodists that played good defense. They had no stars but played hard as a tight unit.

Rome and I were so excited about this game we were almost out of control. Yet we knew that once we touched the basketball in the first few seconds, we would come back to earth. Epworth probably felt the same excitement. We couldn't worry about them but make certain we were ready to play.

Our uniforms were red and black. Epworth's colors were blue and gold. It was the last game of the season and I had never even noticed the colors of any team's uniforms until now. It was an indication of how hyped-up I was.

At half time we led 21 – 17. It wasn't a great lead, but we were confident. We had not played well in the first half, but still had that small lead. Everyone was confident that we would increase the lead in the second half with great play. The third quarter buzzer sounded. The second half would begin in thirty seconds.

Rome came to my side, "Jim," he whispered, "I really gotta use the little boys' room. I'll have a terrible time if I keep waiting."

"Well, don't wait! Go use the restroom. Coach will take you out for a few minutes."

"No, I don't wanna do that!"

"What's the matter with you?"

"If he takes me out, I might not get back in. I'm not takin' any chances."

"Rome, you're crazy! He'll put you back in the game as soon as you come back."

Rome broke off the conversation and walked back on the court. He took no chances of our coach leaving him out. The buzzer sounded and both teams returned to the floor.

The second half started fast and we traded baskets with them three times. Then Butch Berger hit a long one and we were ahead by six. Rome stole a pass and was dribbling the length of the court. No one was going to catch him and with his lay-up, we would be up by eight.

An unbelievable thing then happened. He did not dribble to the basket for a lay-up. He stumbled slightly and banged into the door that led downstairs to the lockers and restrooms. He continued right on downstairs and right out of the game. The ball rolled out of bounds and was awarded to Epworth. Our coach immediately called time out and had us regroup.

"Jim," yelled our coach, "what's Rome doin'? What did he say to you? Is he sick, or what?"

"He said he really had to use the boys' room."

"Why didn't he call time out? We have three time outs left! That was crazy what he did."

"I can't tell you why he did it."

The coach turned to the scorekeeper and brought in Patterson for Rome. "Bring the ball up court with Ryhal."

Patterson was a good kid and a pretty good player, but he was a weak replacement for Rome. After only a few minutes our lead was down to four points. We traded baskets several times, but at the end of the third quarter we held only a two-point lead.

Rome had never come back up the stairs to play again. In fact, he never returned at all. The game continued to slip away and at the end we fell to Epworth 43 – 40. The loss was a bitter pill and a sad end to our season. We felt that if Rome had returned, we would've won, but he didn't return. Our opponents played hard and it wasn't their fault that Rome had mysteriously disappeared. They celebrated long and hard—they deserved the win.

After the game I immediately went down to the locker room to find Rome. I couldn't find him, but found a custodian. "Where's the kid who ran down here at half time to use the restroom? Has he gone already?"

The custodian began to laugh. "You got it all wrong, kid. He didn't run down here—he fell down here, the whole way, the whole twenty-five steps."

"Are you jokin'?"

"No, I'm not. I'm sorry, it's not really funny, but the way he came crashin' down here looked funny at the time. I just couldn't help but laugh."

"But when did he leave?"

"He didn't exactly leave—they came and got him. They took him to the hospital. He broke his kneecap and tore up his knee."

Poor Rome. We thought he'd run down the stairs to the restroom. When he stumbled, he had fallen and crashed through the door all the way to the locker room.

•   •   •

Two days later I visited Rome at the hospital. His room was the very last one on the right side of the newly built hospital wing. The new wing smelled fresh and very hygienic. My shoes squeaked on the newly-waxed floor.

Rome was sleeping as I stopped at the foot of his bed. I stood quietly several minutes, uncertain of what to do. As I turned to leave the room, Rome awakened.

"Jim, don't leave! You're not leavin', are you?"

"I was going to look for a nurse. I wanted to ask if it was okay to wake you. I didn't want to do the wrong thing. I just didn't know what to do."

"You can stay, I was just taking a little nap. I'm okay now, except that this darn knee really hurts."

"Can't they give you somethin' for the pain?"

"They have given me somethin' but it doesn't seem to help."

"How long are you gonna be in here?"

"Only a week. But then I won't be able to do much at home, I'll probably have to lay around for a week at home also."

"I'll come over to see ya, every day if you want me to."

A smile came to Rome's face. It was the first smile he'd shown since I'd come. "Jim, I want you to tell the team how bad I feel about that game. I know I helped lose it. It was my fault and we coulda won that game if I had been there."

"That's not true, Rome. It wasn't your fault. Anyone could've stumbled and fallen down those stairs. It coulda happened to any one of us."

"I should've called time out and used the boys' room when you told me to. But I had to do it my way and that's what happened. That's why it was my fault."

"Cut it out, Rome! I don't wanta hear ya say that. If you don't stop that, I'm gonna leave and go home."

"The only time I felt good since I've been here is when I was thinking about Bum and that whole Popeye affair."

"What do you mean?"

"I really loved that Popeye bout with Bum and all of us takin' on Hostettler's gang. I never liked Hostettler, his dog, or his friends."

"You're right, that was an exciting day."

"I wish you could've brought Bum. I'd really like to see him."

"I did bring him."

"Are you kidding? You can't sneak a dog into the hospital. If you brought him with you, where is he?"

"He's tied to that little crabapple tree just outside your window. He's only about thirty feet away."

"You're crazy."

"Well, if I am, then who owns that black and tan dog tied right out there?"

Rome's eyes opened wide with amazement for several seconds. Then he twisted his body to his left so that he could look through the lone window in his room. There was Bum in plain view. He lay quietly on the grass, looking back at us through the window as if he knew we were talking about him.

"Please bring him in," Rome said.

"Rome, I can't smuggle him into your room. I could never walk past the nurse's station at the front door with a dog."

"You can bring him in, don't use the front door. There's an exit door right outside my room at the end of this hallway. Use that door, then you can slip right into the room. I'm sure you can do it."

"That exit door will lock when I go out and close it. I won't be able to get back inside."

"Take this book and put it so the door won't completely close. If anyone comes in the room and sees Bum, tell them you're just leavin' and take him out the same exit."

Two minutes later I entered Rome's hospital room and thank goodness Bum was practicing his very best behavior. He recognized Rome immediately, went to his bed and jumped up, placing his front paws on the bed with his tail wagging steadily.

"Thanks, Jim, for bringing him in. I really appreciate it. I'm so glad to see you, Bum," said Rome.

My friend placed both his arms around Bum's neck. He held him tightly and began to cry.

I'd never seen Rome cry before. I'd never seen anyone in our gang cry before. I realized it was a compliment to me and especially to Bum.

"I'm sorry, Jim. I'm sorry to cry like this—I just can't help it."

"It's okay, Rome. I'm not troubled by it and I don't want you to be. It's a real compliment to Bum."

"I feel so alone in this hospital. My knee hurts and nothing seems to help. The thought of being here a whole week really gets me down. I'm so sorry I'm crying like this."

"It's okay, Rome."

Through all Rome's grief and crying, Bum never moved. A lesser dog might've tried to get down. A smaller dog might've felt he was being choked to death. Bum never moved. He knew he was helping Rome. He knew Rome was grieving and that he needed something from him.

Rome limped from that fall for the rest of his life. Twenty-five years later, Rome's oldest son asked his dad how he had injured his knee. Rome simply said that it was from a basketball game a long time ago.

There was something very unreal about that entire affair. It had started as a basketball game. Then it seemed like just a humorous fall. It continued as a tragic injury that lasted a lifetime. But for me, it ended with Bum comforting my friend.

Rome really loved Bum. I always knew the other three in our gang liked Bum, but now I knew that perhaps Rome cared for him the most.

Rome continued to hold him by the neck and Bum never tried to move. The dog's perception was almost unbelievable. Bum knew that Rome was hurting badly and needed his comfort. He knew it completely. He knew.

Chapter XVII

There is something wonderful about that last day of the school year that is buried into the mind of every kid. It doesn't matter whether it a second- or third-grader or a senior in high school—the joy is great. It doesn't matter whether it is a boy or girl, each kid has the excitement of looking forward to three months of unplanned excitement. There would be no more trips to the library, no more homework, and no more detention. At least, there would be no more for the next ninety days.

There was only one kid in front of me as I walked home. The young man was nearly two blocks ahead of me and setting a brisk pace. Slowly he pulled away from me, walking faster than I wanted to. I meandered down Scotland Lane, almost aimlessly. I glanced behind and there was not a single student behind me. The young man in front of me turned left down a small street and now I was alone.

The day was wonderful. It was going to be warm but not too hot. There were no clouds in the sky and a very small breeze was stirring.

Birds were singing and a male cardinal landed on someone's lawn. I stopped and looked at him, admiring his beautiful color. He pecked at some seeds in the grass, then flew away. Again I started my journey and frightened a rabbit. From a small thick hedge, he emerged at top speed and darted across the street. I watched his little white tail bob up and down as he left the street and disappeared around a white house. Everything was alive and it made me feel alive also.

An old Ford truck moved down the street where the cottontail had been. I watched it grow smaller as it traveled down the street and out of sight. It was the first vehicle I'd seen since leaving school.

My friends had all headed home before me. Why I was the last one to leave school I do not know—I was usually the first or one of the first, but not today. I was happy walking slowly and especially being alone.

Charlie wanted us to play tennis tomorrow on his clay court. We probably would. Charlie was the best player, since it was his family court that we all used. The rest of us were gaining on him in our tennis skills. Occasionally Will and I had beaten him and Johnny at doubles. Rome liked to play tennis, but tomorrow he simply wanted to play baseball. He was trying to round up some other kids so we would have a baseball game later in the week. Some days we even played triple-headers at baseball. I didn't much care what we played—I enjoyed either game.

I turned the corner on Round Street and was glad. I was getting a little tired and it was only two blocks to home. I would have lunch soon.

At the bottom of the hill on Round Street I stopped. By this time I was only a block from home and the hill was steep, so I stopped to rest.

The hill was green now, but in six months it would be white again for sledding. The warm day helped me think of tennis, baseball and the creek. The snow would have to wait its turn.

I started again, took a big breath and kept going. My walk was a little tougher now because of the hill.

I glanced to my right towards the small stream that was flowing at the bottom of the hill. Something brown was near the tiny blue stream, then it was gone from my view. I took three more steps and saw it again. This time I stopped.

What is that thing, I wondered. The little stream was blue and the grass was green. Therefore the object was easily noticeable from the street. It was too big for a rabbit. It must be a deer. That's it! It's a deer! It had probably gone to the stream to drink.

For several minutes I stood in the middle of the street and watched, but the deer never moved. If it had been drinking, it had surely stopped now. It probably had seen me and was lying motionless.

This was an obvious trick that deer often used. They lie motionless and let people walk right past them. Will's father had told us that many times. Today, however, I was going to wait him out, regardless of how long it took.

I stood motionless in the street. Only my breathing and the blinking of my eyes showed any movement. I was completely silent and was very glad that no cars came my way, for I stood exactly in the middle of the street.

After what I guessed to be about five minutes, I decided to wait no longer. Slowly I walked toward the deer and wondered if it was a buck or a doe. In a short time I would have the answer to my question. I moved very slowly and quietly toward it.

As I got closer to the animal I could see it was rather small. Perhaps it was a fawn and the doe was nearby. Surely it could smell me now—I was only twenty feet away.

But it was not a deer—it was a dog. It was not brown, but black and tan. It looked like it could be—it was—it was Bum!

I hurried to where he was. He lay motionless with his muzzle only a few inches from the small stream. Obviously, he had come to drink. Was he injured? Was he sick? Had he been hit by a car?

"Bum!" I called. "Bum! Here, boy, it's me. Bum, get up, boy."

With my fingers, I pushed his shoulder. I pushed him again, only this time very hard. He was not sick and he was not injured. He was dead.

Maybe this wasn't Bum! Maybe he just looked like my dog. That's it, he just looked like Bum. He obviously belonged to someone else. He'd probably been struck by a car, came here when he was injured, and died. This wasn't Bum!

I tried hard to believe he belonged to someone else. I couldn't believe he was Bum. My mind worked hard; I just couldn't believe it. But the brown leather collar with his license showed it was my dog.

"Bum, get up! I need you, boy. Bum, get up! Get up, I need you!"

I screamed with all my strength and my voice echoed from the little hill. I felt if I yelled loud enough and long enough, his spirit would return and he would get up. But he didn't get up. He would never get up—he was gone.

A terrible feeling ran through me as I felt those words. I sat on the soft grass only a few inches from him. My father had told me to tie him to the henhouse. I was careless and Bum had paid the price. He surely had been poisoned and had come to the stream to drink. My father had warned me, but I had not listened. I began to cry bitterly.

I had felt that he would be with me for many years—thirteen, fourteen, or more. Will and I had made many plans for running rabbits and shooting pheasants with him. But our plans were not meant to be. I had had him only two years. We had lived in the moment. Now he was gone.

At last I stopped crying. For an hour I sat quietly with him. The thought of going home without him was too terrible.

With my fingers I began to dig his grave. I would not leave him in the grass this way. My fingers began to hurt, but no matter—I kept digging. I found an old iron pipe and used it. My hands were now bleeding and the old pipe helped greatly.

Deeper and deeper I dug. I wanted him completely covered. No marauding varmint would find him. At last the hole was complete.

I laid him carefully in his grave. His eyes were closed and he looked at peace. But when I covered him with the loose dirt, I felt destroyed. Again I cried—this time, uncontrollably. The more I covered him, the more I cried. With both hands I smoothed the dirt over him. At last it was over and I stopped crying.

Two small logs were nearby. I pulled them over the fresh dirt and covered the remainder of the new dirt with grass and flowers.

I looked around for some kind of stone—some marker. I walked around the hill, but could find nothing that was large enough. In the stream below

I found the right one. It was too heavy for me to carry and so I pushed it slowly up the hill a few feet. I breathed heavily and stopped to rest. A few minutes later, I reached the soft dirt. Into the very center of it I rolled the stone. Then I stood on the stone, forcing it partially down into the earth.

It was time to go. My mother was probably wondering where I was. When I was about half-way back to Round Street, I looked back one last time. My face was a mess, my hands were bleeding, and my clothes were very dirty, but it was over. Thank God in Heaven, it was over.

Chapter XVIII

It was a good day to have a pleasant drive. I drove slowly; I was in no hurry. I had no idea what the speed limit was, and I didn't care. I knew I was well below it.

A bright red convertible moved away from my truck and in about twenty seconds was gone from view. Turning the corner onto Round Street, I slowed even more. I examined each house as I passed it. Some houses I didn't recognize at all. Some houses had changed a little, but others looked almost exactly the same as they did many years ago.

The truck drifted slowly to a stop in front of the last house, just before the bottom of the hill. I didn't want to drive it any farther. At the very bottom of the hill the road was very narrow, too narrow for anyone to park and leave room for two lanes of traffic.

I closed the driver's door and stood next to my gray truck for several minutes. It would be my last trip to this place. It had been nearly seventy years since I had been to the bottom of the hill with him.

Very slowly I came upon the little stream that trickled at the bottom of the hill and then traveled under the road. The stream would guide me to the spot.

Trees of all shapes and sizes were everywhere. Some of them were three feet thick at the trunk. Heavy vines tried to block my path. The place had changed greatly and there would be no sledding on this hill now. The kids would have to go sled-riding somewhere else, if they went sled-riding at all any more.

Only thirty feet into the little forest and I was lost already. I looked back to where I thought Round Street was, but I couldn't see it. There seemed to be nothing but trees. The only thing that saved me was the hill itself. I knew at the bottom of the hill was the stream that continued to flow. Slowly and very carefully I started down the hill. I grabbed tiny trees as I made my way. I walked slowly; at this stage of my life I did not need a broken ankle.

After a short time I reached the bottom and could hear the stream. It made only a small trickling noise, but I could hear it clearly.

The stream flowed to the avenue and I knew where I was now. I followed it slowly, not wanting to slip on the tiny bank.

It's an interesting thing about growing older. Sometimes I can't remember what happened an hour earlier, but I can remember clearly what happened sixty or seventy years ago. That's how it was about that spot.

I looked around the ground and found it. It was the stone I'd placed there many years earlier. The stone had sunk into the ground a little more and was covered with a little grass, but I was sure. On the soft ground I sat next to the shiny granite. Directly beneath me, I knew he lay where I had placed him.

The last time I had seen this stone was almost seventy years ago. Yet in my mind, I had been here many times. Through all the years he had been with me. Through all the years I had remembered that day. A thousand times I had remembered that day. But by God's goodness, I had learned to forgive myself.

I talked to him out loud as if he were right here. Of course he wasn't here, and yet—he was here. He was not with me, and yet he would always be with me.

"This will be the last time I'll be seeing you, Bum. The old gang is all gone now, except you and me. Maybe you know and maybe you don't, but I wanted to stop and tell you. There's been a lot of water under the bridge.

"Charlie Rudolph died about ten years ago up near Meadville. You remember Charlie? He had the tennis court on Moore Avenue. We had to tie you up to the apple tree behind the court. You would always steal the tennis balls during our game. You couldn't tolerate any kind of ballgame going on around you unless you got to play, too.

"Charlie was on his way to a tennis match to see his granddaughter play. Some older woman crossed the center line and hit his car. Charlie was killed instantly and she didn't get a scratch. He was a good guy–I miss him.

"Johnny McCann went west. Colorado or California, I'm not sure. Johnny earned a PhD from Pitt. He went on to be a school superintendent of one of the largest school districts in that state. We always knew he was a smart guy. He passed on about five or six years ago. A good fellow—I miss him, too.

"Rome Beltrone was killed in some sort of an accident, a fall, I think. He lived in Erie. I don't know if he fell at home or at work. It was a strange fall. At least, he died quickly and he didn't suffer. I knew Rome since before first grade.

"Will Franklin died just last year. It was a heart attack. You knew Will pretty well. I went to his house that first day you came by and I found you.

"I grieved a lot the week he died. I simply had to talk to someone about it and so I called my daughter-in-law in Ohio. She was always a good listener and she helped me. Will's sister called me and gave me the sad news. He was my best friend.

"I better be going now. I got a good distance to go. They'll be expecting me at home. I just stopped over to say 'Goodbye'.

"So long, Bum. There will not be another come along like you in a long time – perhaps never again. So, wherever you are, I hope you have a lot of friends and I hope the fishing is good.

"It sure would be great to bump into you again; we'd have a lot of memories to share. I'll keep a sharp eye out for you out near the old Henderson farm and near the patch of woods behind the henhouse. Most of all, I'll look for you near the creek, in some little inlet or cove, where the water is cold."

• • •

Two years later, James W. Ryhal died on February 13, 1997, in the State of Indiana. He was eighty-four.